WHO WERE THE PRE-COLUMBIANS?

To Paglene & Jim,
good friends - great seafarers
On board the "Century"
03/13/03 -

Sincerely
BB Kaufman

WHO WERE THE PRE-COLUMBIANS?

*Mysteries, Adventures and Challenges
for Today's World*

With Illustrations and Photographs

by
Bernard Barken Kaufman

New World Art Inc.
Publisher
1993

WHO WERE THE PRE-COLUMBIANS?

Grateful Appreciation and Acknowledgments to Directors of The National Museum and The Museum of Archaeology and Anthropology, Lima, Peru

Book Design and Typography: Jeff Farr
Illustrations: Marius Sznajderman
Cover Photographs: Pam Farr

First edition, Library of Congress Catalogue Number: 92-062495

ISBN No. 0-9635235-0-3

Published by New World Art Inc.
P.O. Box 3486
Pinehurst, NC 28374
Tel: 919-295-3727 (after 1/1/94, 910-295-3727)

Printed by Sparks Press, Raleigh, N.C.

Other works
by

BERNARD BARKEN KAUFMAN

executive producer of
eight documentary films presented
at The New York Film Festival
including three award-winning films
one a Gold Medal

For my wife
Phyllis Rohm Kaufman

Shard from a Barrancoid burial urn. Collection of the author.
Photo: J. Fabry

CONTENTS

PREFACE
October 12, 1492

Latin Americans call Columbus Day "Dia de la Raza," which in Spanish means "Day of the Human Race." Historians claim the name given by the Spanish clergy refers to the arrival of the first human beings in the Americas. This belief stems from the conquistadores, who considered the Indians a sub-species, not really human. Cortez and Pizarro were convinced that it was their God-given duty to bring the Indians into the church and were not averse to using the methods of the Inquisition in so doing.

The atrocities perpetrated upon the Indians in the name of religion are clearly revealed in engravings by the Spanish friars who documented the conquest of the Aztecs and the Incas. The European search for gold was camouflaged by a deep-rooted and blinding religious fervor. Today, the Latin American faithful celebrate Columbus Day by going to church.

Columbus Day commemorates the arrival of the first white men in the Americas, and "Dia de la Raza" refers to those famous Caucasians. I find it paradoxical that it is celebrated by Latin Americans, who themselves are such a mixture of races, including to a large extent, the Indian.

The year 1992 marked the 500th anniversary of the landing of Columbus in America, acknowledged throughout the world as an important historical event, yet one which led to infamous consequences. The arrival of Europeans started the large scale debasement and almost complete extinction of the indigenous inhabitants of the Western Hemisphere.

Bishop Bartolome de las Casas, an eyewitness to 40 years

of Spanish atrocities in the New World, in 1552 wrote his book entitled "A Relation of the First Voyages and Discoveries Made by the Spaniards in America and an Account of Their Unparalleled Cruelties Upon the Indians":

"They baptize them, then enslave them and send them in chains to work in the fields and in the mines...The Almighty seems to have inspired these people with a weakness and softness of humor, like the lambs, and the Spaniards have fallen upon them so fiercely, they resemble savage tigers, lions and wolves, ravaged with a passing hunger...They applied themselves 40 years wholly to the massacre of the poor wretches, putting them to all kinds of torments and punishments, to reduce their people from 3,000,000 to less than 300. (From 50,000,000 to 1,000,000 is closer to reality for the entire Western Hemisphere.)

When the governor of Cuba wanted to assign him Mexican land for colonization, Cortez replied, "I have come to find gold for the crown, not to plow the fields like a peasant!" Recent research reveals that between 25 and 30 million Indians were exterminated in Latin America, all in the name of gold, which the Indians called the "Christian god."

The directive for the conquest of the Americas came from Europe, a conquest which transformed men into avaricious monsters. This book is written for their victims, those courageous, often maligned and misunderstood people who were living in the New World on October 12, 1492, and to their ancestors, the pre-Columbians, the real discoverers of America.

B.B. Kaufman

A NOTE TO THE READER
The Author and Archaeology

The Brooklyn Museum in New York houses one of the world's finest collections of Egyptology, comparable to that of the British Museum and surpassed only by the National Museum of Cairo. During my boyhood years I was fortunate to live within a half-hour bicycle ride to this outstanding institution, and visits to the museum became my regular Saturday morning expedition. On rainy days I took the subway, provided I had the twenty-cent fare.

It is understandable that an impressionable youth, under those special conditions, could easily become interested in archaeology. I spent so many hours among the ancient mummies lying in their painted sarcophagi, that I came to know them all by name. I would walk deep inside the dimly lighted tombs, at times sketching the hieroglyphics on the stone walls which had been transplanted from the desert, block by block, to the grand Egyptian Hall of the museum. Not all the glyphs were translated, and I worked hard to decipher those that weren't, sometimes inventing unbelievably fantastic stories. After all these years, I can recall the balmy aroma of musk which incredibly still clung to the stones; an ever-so-faint scent had remained after 3000 years of exposure to the wind and sun of the desert.

It could be considered unusual for one so young to have taken such a keen interest in a subject as esoteric as archaeology. However, this special concern did not detract in any way from my love for the boyhood pursuits of baseball, flying model airplanes and just being with friends. I realize now that I was a little different from the other boys on the block. Although I traded Street & Smith's "War Aces" magazines with them and played on the local stick-ball and handball teams, I was the only one whose favorite person was Dr. Roy Chapman Andrews, the famous paleontologist, anthropologist and dinosaur hunter. Also, unlike the others, I spent many hours reading my way through the fantastic adventures of Peter Freuchen, Knud Rassmussen, Robert E. Peary and Richard E. Byrd. I remember once asking my father what he thought of my becoming an explorer, and I can still hear his incredulous, laconic reply, "Son, how are you going to earn a living?"

In later life, and during thirty years of residing in South America, my interest turned to the pre-Columbians, the ancient Americans who contributed so much to the world's civilization, yet did not leave a written language. I believe that my attraction to those old cultures is derived precisely from the fact that they did not have an alphabetical language, and in order to learn about them, the only alternative was to study their architecture and ceramics. All my life I have been intrigued by the artifacts left behind by the pre-Columbians. It has always been a thrill for me to unearth a piece of their history and thereby close the gap of thousands of years which existed between us. I know that those prehistoric people, through their ceramic pots and sculpture, through the remains of their cities, temples and tombs, will always be with me, always pique my curiosity and challenge me to open new investigative paths.

INTRODUCTION

This is a story about survival. A story of people with indomitable courage and enormous spirit, who survived a journey which took 12,000 years, covered three continents and populated a hemisphere. They were the pre-Columbians, the inhabitants of the Americas before Columbus landed on its shores.

The word pre-Columbian is a generalization, and refers to all the Indians who lived in the Western Hemisphere at the time of, and before, the arrival of Columbus. The names by which we know them, Inca, Chimú, Nazca, Moche, are Quechua names, given to them by their descendants. Those which are not Quechua were invented by the Spanish conquerors, who named the Indians after the places in which they were found. We do not know what those ancient people actually called themselves, since few of them left written languages, and most of them disappeared before the time of the Conquest.

The pre-Columbians arrived around 12,000 years ago, give or take a thousand years, during the last ice age, over a land bridge which connected Asia to Alaska, crossing what is now known as the Bering Sea. This land bridge was not a narrow corridor, as many conceive bridges to be, but was instead an extensive stretch of land about 500 miles wide, almost as wide as the Alaskan peninsula. Because of the extreme cold brought on by the ice age, the waters froze and retreated, causing the sea's level to drop. As the water froze it was trapped in ice, and the sea contracted, exposing thousands of square miles of land which lay beneath it. This became the passageway over which man travelled into the Americas.

The land bridge is no longer there. The water swelled with the warming of the atmosphere and returned to its present level; but the bridge remained long enough to enable people to migrate from Asia to the North American continent. The north-south migration theory expounds that there is a direct link between those early arrivals from Asia and all the later Indian cultures of the Americas, and that humans did not evolve in the Western Hemisphere from Paleolithic origins as they did in Europe, Asia and Africa.

This is, however, only one theory among many concerning the origin of humans in the New World. There are still anthropologists combing the surface of the earth of the Americas trying to disprove the north-south migration idea, claiming that man did evolve in the Western Hemisphere, just as he had in other parts of the world. There are even some who propose that man's origin was actually in the New World, and that he migrated north, across the land bridge to populate Asia and Europe. In effect, a reverse migration. While all geologists, anthropologists and archaeologists agree that the land bridge existed, what has to be decided is the direction in which it was crossed!

It is difficult to believe that a south-to-north migration could have taken place, since the Ice Age glaciers moved from north to south, producing the ferocious blast of cold which killed all the grasses and drove the grazing herds in a southerly direction.

Also, up to this moment no real evidence has been uncovered to support claims that the existing indigenous groups are the result of an evolutionary process which took place in the New World. Not a single human fossil —bone or tooth — has ever been found to indicate that Paleolithic man or his predecessors, classified as homo erectus, existed anywhere in the Americas. Nothing comparable to Neanderthal Man, or Pithecanthropus, or Cro-Magnon, as were discovered in other parts of the world. Up to the present time, in the New World, not a single sign. Nothing.

The evidence which supports the north to south land bridge migration theory is a definite physiological link between the pre-Columbians and their Asian ancestors, the same connection apparent between modern day western world Indians and the people who inhabit the steppes of Asia. The similarities in stature, skin and hair color, shape of the eyes, all indicate that those who arrived in the Americas with the Ice Age belonged to the Mongolian race and are a further indication that the Asia to Alaska migration must have taken place. While we cannot conclusively prove this, up to now no better explanation has been given for the arrival of early man in the Western Hemisphere. I shall therefore hold to this theory, and make it my guide in writing this book.

What happened to those Ice Age travellers who arrived in the Americas after that arduous journey, into a land where no human had ever been? How did they live? How did they establish some of the most interesting and complex cultures ever known, and why did most of them disappear?

As the answers to these questions unfold, it will become obvious to the reader that those migrants did not remain the simple hunter-gatherers they were when they arrived, but developed instead into societies of peoples whose extraordinary accomplishments and inventiveness made a great mark upon the world.

Pre-Columbian Gifts to Europe

What a great variety of agricultural products used today actually originated with the pre-Columbian Indian! Few understand the heights their civilization reached and how much we owe them. The Spanish conquerors however, were quick to learn from New World techniques, especially in agriculture.

Arriving in the Americas with a belief in white, European superiority, Cortez and Pizarro were embarrassed when they encountered the sophisticated life-style of the Indians. Nevertheless, they didn't hesitate to sail back across the Atlantic with all the products and ideas acquired from them, together with many shiploads of pilfered gold and silver.

Although called Irish potatoes, the common potato did not originate in Ireland. The inhabitants of the British Isles were living in the Stone Age at the time the pre-Columbians were cultivating over 30 varieties of potato in the highlands of the Andes, employing elaborate terracing and irrigation methods. They cultivated corn, the basic maize, the most important contributor to the growth of large, complex pre-Columbian agricultural societies. These American Indian cultures were first to produce coffee and chocolate, first to grow tomatoes, peppers, strawberries, peanuts and squash, none of which existed in Europe prior to the Spanish Conquest. The Indians gave us tobacco, rubber, medicinal herbs and dyestuffs. They also provided us with superb examples of what can happen to civilized societies as the result of overpopulation, overdependence on agriculture and a sedentary existence.

MIGRATION
The Land Bridge Theory

Migration — A Fantasy

The Ice Age came down fast upon the land, killing most living creatures and dispersing those that remained alive. The extreme cold which descended from the north polar cap was borne on a wind which froze everything in its path. The lush green land of the Asian steppes was turned into hardened tundra and then to ice in the face of the approaching glacier, forcing every living thing to flee southward.

They sought the sun, the warmth, the nourishing vegetation. They were driven by a terrible hunger — first the big ones, the mammoth and mastodon, the musk ox and bison, the caribou and all the other herbivorous creatures still able to escape. Behind these came the carnivores, the predators and scavengers, the lion and tiger, jaguar and puma, wild dogs and wolves and jackals. Then followed the greatest predator of all, man, the two-legged one who could outrun every animal over a long distance. Built for the hunt and able to cover many miles without tiring, he had the greatest intelligence and had learned to fashion weapons. He was small compared to most of the animals he hunted; only five feet in height, deep chested and muscular, with copper-colored skin and straight, black hair and black epicanthic eyes.

Around 12,000 B.C., two migrating creatures had sought refuge in a cave. These two, a man and a woman were the sole survivors of their clan. Even their two young children had died.

He awakened to feel the body of the women huddled against his side. There was little protection against the night cold except the warmth they provided one another.

He closed his eyes once more and could hear the wind as it continued to howl outside. In the distance the sound of the glacier was like the rumbling stomachs of a gigantic herd of grazing bison. The snow covered everything during the night. They had no fire...they had seen neither wood nor tinder for a long time.

She went outside looking for lichens under the snow. She remembered bison foraging for this tough grass, which could be eaten to provide some nourishment, enough to keep from starving. It was so long since there was any fresh-killed meat, the real provider and sustainer of life, so necessary, yet now so difficult to find.

Ice formed in her eyes and nostrils, and when she breathed deeply the air tore at her lungs with a burning ferocity. How easy it would be, she thought, to lie down and just go to sleep, as she had seen so many of her people do in the days past, to peacefully go to sleep forever. But no, she had just seen something which told her it was not time for that, not yet time to join the others, because at that moment, something caused her thoughts about death to change completely. She caught sight of familiar indentations in the snow, and her instinct for survival took charge, obliterating all other thoughts. At her feet, tracks! Tracks of an animal! Fresh tracks and spore of a small caribou, one that had apparently become separated from the herd.

She ran into the cave, stumbling on the ice that had formed at the entrance overnight, calling to her man to wake up, to get up and come quickly.

"There are tracks!...tracks in the snow...a caribou...meat!...come quickly...it cannot be far away!"

He heard her faintly through the stupor brought on by

the cold and near starvation. He got up deliberately, his mind slowly absorbing the meaning in her words, and then hastening his movements, he picked up the spear and followed her outside the cave. The gnawing hunger became more apparent to both of them as they set out.

It did not take long to cover the distance between them and their prey, and they saw the animal, a small male caribou, the first in many days. He was tearing at the snow with his hooves, trying to pry out a bit of brown vegetation which lay beneath the frozen ground. They approached with great caution, making no sudden movements. The spear flew swift and sure, with an accuracy of skill and much practice, and the animal fell immediately.

They each took quick turns sucking the blood pouring from the wound and with each swallow felt their strength return and the warmth spread through their bodies. With a stone axe he skinned the animal and cut several pieces of meat which they quickly ate. He then picked up the carcass and put it over his shoulder. It would soon freeze, and they would chop pieces from it as they travelled. They discarded the hide since there was no time to prepare it. Now they had to keep going to find the herd. It could not be too far ahead of them. The herd had to be found if they were to survive.

She picked up the spear from the snow, breaking away some of the blood reddened ice which had adhered to its point, putting some of the ice in her mouth. She handed him the spear and followed closely behind.

The Clovis Point

Before the last ice age, the climate of the steppes of Asia was as warm as the plains of Africa, abundant with the same animals which inhabit the Serengeti today. In addition to the big cats, buffalo and antelope, the plains were also inhabited by the now-extinct mammoth and mastodon. While game was plentiful, it took great skill and endurance for the hunter to successfully track and kill the large mammals. Tracking a 10,000 pound mammoth would take many days, but the effort was undoubtedly worth it, since this would supply the group with enough food for months, and the skins would provide enough clothing for years.

Killing animals as large and powerful as mammoth and mastodon required well-organized and experienced hunters with strength, stamina and special weapons. There was no animal then, nor is there one now, which could outrun a young, well-trained human. Many swift runners among the four-legged animals can easily outrun a person over a short distance, but over a really long distance the human will win. Even the cheetah, considered to be the fastest animal, one which can run 60 miles an hour, would collapse if it were required to run for more than half a mile at a time. A horse must be rested after a two-mile gallop, while a trained athlete is able to run 20 miles or more at one time and is ready to run again in a few days. In ability and stamina, the primitive hunters could be compared to the athletes of today. The hunt consisted simply of running the prey to exhaustion, encircling the animal, and moving in for the kill with spears and clubs.

The special weapon which primitive man possessed, which he began to fashion before the long migration, was

the Clovis point, also called the Paijan point , named because of its discovery, embedded in the fossil bones of
mammoths, at a Clovis, New Mexico, anthropological dig.
The Clovis point was made by chipping away at a piece of
flint until an elongated, fine-pointed, sharp-edged spearhead was attained. With the right piece of flint, the point
could easily be fashioned in a couple of hours, then attached
to the end of a shaft of wood, hewn from a stout limb.
Animal blood was used for glue and sinew for the string
employed to fasten the Clovis point to the wooden shaft.

This spearhead made the difference in establishing man's
superior hunting skills and was in use long before the Iron
Age. The Clovis point gave the primitives exceptional
prowess in the hunt for fresh meat, and without it they
would never have survived the long migration.

Some did not continue southward after crossing the land
bridge but stayed in the extreme north, notwithstanding
the cold weather. They found what they were looking for
— large numbers of mammals in the sea and on the ice floes.
The nomadic hunters were able to live well, with the seal
and whale and walrus providing rich meat and fat, thick
furs and good hides. They kept their population low, of
necessity, adjusting to the food supply and to the fierce climate as they moved over the enormous, white expanse of
the Arctic.

At first they hunted on foot and later trained teams of
dogs which pulled their sleds swiftly over the ice. When
the ice broke up, they fashioned kayaks from which to kill
the seal, walrus and whale.

Some of those Arctic hunters followed the caribou herds
on their migration to the south and stayed with them in the
more temperate lands. In the heavily wooded forests of the

vast North American continent, where the seasons were more defined, where there was abundance of game, and the trees were full of birds. Here also were swift-running rivers whose waters descended from the melting glacier in the north, rivers which were filled with fish all year.

The migration did not take place quickly. It took thousands of years for the descendants of those who crossed the land bridge to reach the South American continent. Nor was the movement of the migrants always in a steady north-to-south direction. Backtracking and crisscrossing, the hunters followed the movement of the herds. What kept the migrants going was their adaptability to environmental change and their instinctive consciousness of two basic needs, self-preservation and the satisfaction of never-ending hunger.

The life of those early people was confined to the requirements of their clan and the demands of the hunt. Those with whom they lived and hunted and travelled were "the people," the only ones of importance. They were the family, the protection; and as the clan grew, it developed into the tribe. Each member was completely dependent upon the tribe, because the hunt needed organization, unity, and a fundamental trust in the people, if it were to be successful. The clan or tribe furnished those needs. The outsiders, the strangers, were considered inferior, because they were not of "the people."

By the year 10,000 B.C., the North American Indians became settlers, and their former wanderings ceased. They moved across the continent and took over lands where living conditions were suitable. There were those who reached the southwestern deserts of Arizona and became the Cochise, the first farmers of the Americas. While this was taking place, other groups moved eastward to the Ohio valley, where they became the ingenious Moundbuilders, whose large and numerous mounds were shrines in which they buried the bodies of their rulers. These were the first people on the continent to establish a real agrarian society, the first to build cities. The Adena culture of southern Ohio, Indiana and Kentucky built thousands of mounds, many of which have been investigated by archaeologists.

At about the same time, Arizona and New Mexico were inhabited by cultures which built cities suspended on the sides of cliffs. One group was the Anasazi, "the ancient ones" in the Navajo language, builders of a complex society of cliff dwellers; others were the cliff people of the Chaco Canyon, Mesa Verde and Pueblo Bonito. Their sun bleached cities stand today empty, fragile, white adobe brick structures, carved into the sides of canyon walls, bordering on the reservations of the Navajo and Hopi.

During the development of the southwestern cultures, the Indian tribes of North America were becoming established. In the west: the Kwakiutl, Chinook, Yurok, Blackfoot, Arapaho, Kiowa, Paiute, Mohave, Flathead. In the central plains: the Pawnee, Mandan, Dakota, Crow, Sioux, Osage, Iowa, Cheyenne, Shawnee. Around the Great Lakes region the Patawatomi, Erie, Huron, Ojibwa; in the northeast the Iroquois, Delaware, Susquehannok, Powhatan, Cherokee, Creek, Chickasaw; in the southeast the Timuca and Calusa. These are only a few of the several hundred different tribes which inhabited North America at the time of the European discovery.

Because of the large distances which separated them, and because all travel was done on foot, the tribes had little contact with one another. Even tribal warfare from territorial disputes was infrequent. The tribes remained very much apart and developed distinctive customs and languages. In many instances the dialect spoken by the tribe of a certain language group could not be understood by another tribe in the same group. A study of Indian languages traces their migration into Central and South America showing that the Shoshoni of Oklahoma spoke pure Aztec, which adds credence to the north-south migration theory.

The lives of the Indians of North America changed dramatically with the arrival of the white man, with the greatest change of all brought about by the introduction of the horse and the gun. These provided faster and easier means of hunting and they became the Indians' two most prized possessions. Unfortunately they also led to the raiding parties, tribal warfare and the cult of the scalp-taking warrior-hero. Guns and horses traded to the Indians by the whites turned the tribes against one another and caused the eventual devastation of the Indian's principal source of food, the buffalo.

During a period of several thousand years, while the American Indian tribes were becoming established, groups of hunter-gatherers continued the great migration to the south, continually seeking warmer climate and an easier way of life. Some migrated to Mexico, where they became the Toltec, Mixtec and Olmec. Others later developed into the Maya of the Yucatan peninsula, Guatemala, Honduras and Belize. Three thousand years ago, before the Central American cultures came into being, some anthropologists believe a group of hunter-gatherers arrived on the northwestern coast of Peru.

Tribal Rites of Passage

They had lain together wrapped in a buffalo skin, in front of her parents' tepee, so the people of the village would know they were to be married shortly. He recalled the warmth of her body and the softness of her skin, the look in her eyes, but he must not think of those things on this most important day. Their actions had announced to the elders that they wanted to be married, and the elders had agreed that the ceremony would take place in five days. Today was the first day, the day of the sweat lodge where he would attempt to communicate with his spirit, the great condor.

Several of the elders had already gathered in attendance for the sweat lodge ceremony. The shaman arrived, and the young man was given the coral colored, fleshy mushrooms to eat as soon as he entered the lodge. He stepped down into the chest-high pit that had been dug in the ground. Heated rocks were placed around the edges of the pit and two of the elders began pouring water over the rocks, creating clouds of steam, which momentarily seared his skin and prevented him from seeing their faces. He breathed deeply of the steam, gradually becoming light-headed, and overcome by weakness.

The mushrooms were beginning to work, and he slowly lost consciousness. His head started to spin, and he felt as if he were floating upward and leaving his body behind. He could still hear the chanting voices of the elders, faintly penetrating his stupor, and then he saw the large black condor sweep across the sky and fly down over his head. One of the condor's wings brushed lightly across his face, and he knew that this was his spirit which had come to greet him. He was now one with his spirit and he understood that the great condor was in agreement that the marriage take place.

The elders pulled him up from the pit and briskly wiped his body with dry leaves. They gave him a water pouch from which he was allowed to drink deeply; he would have no food or water for four days to come, while he sat on the mountaintop in deep meditation.

MOUNDBUILDERS

Movers of the Earth

MOUNDBUILDERS
Movers of the Earth

The bountiful, magnificent forests described by the pilgrims who landed with the *Mayflower* on the New England coast were not always so bountiful, nor were they always so magnificent. The Pilgrims wrote about the Indians they encountered as "a few primitive creatures, living by hunting and fishing." It is now known that the Indians were not always so few, nor did they always live by hunting and fishing.

A study of Indian burial mounds in the Ohio, Tennessee and Mississippi valleys has uncovered information concerning population on the North American continent at the time the Europeans arrived. Until recently, historians believed that there were approximately 700,000 Indians when Columbus landed in the West Indies in 1492. The latest archaeological investigation of the Moundbuilder culture has revealed that there were at least 20,000,000 Indians in North America, living in complex, agrarian societies.

The mounds of the pre-Columbians dot the landscape of the United States. There are over 10,000 mounds of various shapes and sizes in the Ohio and Tennessee valleys alone, and many more throughout the southeastern part of the country, mounds on the outskirts of small towns, in large cities, national parks and on farms. Mounds have been bulldozed to make way for road construction. Large scale agriculture has flattened and plowed through many. A mound stands in the middle of a golf course in Granville, Ohio.

It has been calculated that it would have required 25,000 well-organized workers to build just one mound...some of the mounds are 100 feet high, 1000 feet in circumference, and contain 500,000 cubic feet of soil. Mound building was large-scale, labor-intensive construction and could have been accomplished only in highly-populated areas.

The Moundbuilders were similar to many of the other pre-Columbian agricultural societies in existence at that time. The people were tied to the land and built large permanent cities to house a sedentary populace. Their religion demanded the construction of temples dedicated to the gods and as a burial place for the royalty. Instead of building temples of adobe brick or stone, the Moundbuilders used tons and tons of earth.

When the ancestors of the Moundbuilders crossed the land bridge 10,000 years before, they brought with them the great social tool — fire. They discovered corn and began the first agrarian society in the Americas. With fire they changed everything. The Indians simply cleared off all the trees, and when the Spaniards arrived, instead of forests, they found extensive tracts of land converted to the cultivation of corn. Thousands of square miles, farmed by hundreds of thousands of workers, provided harvests to feed millions of people.

The large indigenous populations of North America did not last long. Not only were many killed outright by the Europeans, the white man also brought diseases to the Indians for which they had no immunity. Within a few years, smallpox, influenza and cholera had almost completely wiped out the Indian population. Their numbers were so reduced that there weren't enough of them left to farm the land. By the year 1550, driven by hunger, the few survivors reverted to the hunter-gatherer existence.

How is it possible that the Pilgrims, upon landing in the

New World only 128 years after Columbus, encountered such extensive and lush forests, if these forests did not exist when the Spaniards first arrived?

Archaeological studies have made the answer simple. The conquerors had so thoroughly devastated them the Indians were forced to stop the mass cultivation of corn. (The Spaniards did not think corn fit for human consumption.)

The trees were therefore given an opportunity to grow back. It takes only 20 to 25 years for a tree to reach maturity, some species even less, and in soil which was nitrogen- and carbon-enriched by centuries of burning, growth was further accelerated. If the land is left undisturbed, temperate zone forests, where the nutrients go deeply into the soil, will reproduce and flourish under normal climatic conditions.

The principal difference in the cultivation of basic cereal crops between the pre-Columbians and today's North American inhabitants, is that the Indians planted corn to feed themselves, whereas today's corn is planted mostly to feed animals, then the animals are eaten. The pre-Columbians did not have cattle. The first cows and bulls were brought to the New World by the Spaniards at the end of the 15th century, along with horses.

Of the 200,000,000 metric tons of corn grown yearly in the United States today, 120,000,000 tons are used to feed animals, so that less than one-half of the crop is consumed by people. The animals, mostly steers, are grossly inefficient as producers of human food, yet we spend 60% of our food dollar on animal products. It really does not matter that a large portion of the steers are dry-lot fed and are off the range, the land is still needed for the cultivation of corn, which is what feeds the steers, which wind up in our supermarkets as neatly packaged cuts of meat. Cows are permitted to live a lot longer, and during their productive lifetime, consume even more tonnage of corn than do steers, in order to provide for the tremendous quantities of dairy products demanded.

Cattle cannot be raised successfully without a large supply of water. A steer will consume 7,000 gallons of water from birth to slaughter, a period of 18-20 months, and dairy cattle twenty times that amount. For these reasons the underground water supply in the plains states is disappearing rapidly. The more the production of beef and dairy products is accelerated, the more the water level goes down. Unlike the Goajiro Indians of Venezuela, who have learned to live with the rainy seasons and lead their cattle to the water supply in different parts of their land, the American cattle grower cannot rely upon a single rainy season, does not move cattle from place to place, and the animals continually deplete the water resources.

Like the pre-Columbians of North America, present-day farmers in North and South America continue to slash and burn the forests. In the tropical zone, the land beneath the forest is nutrient poor and subject to erosion. The trees do not grow back after they are cut down. Today's forests in many parts of the world are burned or otherwise devastated to make way for agricultural land or to provide woodpulp for paper and timber for lumber. The redwood forests of California and the rain forests of the Amazon are examples of this destruction of natural resources.

Forests produce rain and oxygen. The more trees cut down, the less rainfall, and the more the water supply diminishes, the less oxygen is released into the atmosphere.

AZTEC

The Innovators

AZTEC
Cortez Invades

The wide acceptance of European religion by the indigenous inhabitants of Latin America has been looked upon by historians as a cross-culturalization or a cross-fertilization. I believe this a spurious assumption, since large numbers of the present-day inhabitants of Latin America are for the most part considered to belong to a separate "bronze" race, notwithstanding the fact that many are mestizos. The pre-Columbian ancestors of these people were forced to accept the Christian, European god. The Europeans accepted nothing of social or spiritual value from the Indians.

Those who escaped the sword of the Spaniards and the few who survived after the scourge of conquistador diseases had no choice but to acknowledge the omnipotence of one supreme deity whom they no doubt considered more powerful than their many gods. And so it has remained to this day. Millions of descendants of those conquered South and Central Americans not only cling to the church of the Spaniards, Italians and Portuguese, they have become its most devoted and stalwart followers.

The religious parades which take place in the plazas of cities all over Latin America on holy days bear witness to this. The people whose looks are so decidedly Aztec, Maya and Inca, carry the painted, heavy wood and plaster images of saints from the gold-emblazoned altars of churches and cathedrals and parade them to the sounds of drums and trumpets. The crowds of men and women holding lighted candles in the evening hours wait for the mass to begin, hypnotized by the loud tolling of church bells and the heavy aroma of incense. Young men and women consider this a social time accepted by everyone. Old men with small feathers pinned to the hair on the back of their heads, wear colorful serapes and mantas. Women crowd the streets with sleeping babies tucked into rebozos — woven Indian shawls — tied across their backs.

This is the ultimate anachronism. They have given up the old gods, but most of them have not given up the old ways. Many in Peru, Ecuador and Bolivia still speak Quechua. They have not forgotten the ancient system of slash and burn planting and harvesting. They still grow the hot chili peppers, hand grind the corn as did their ancestors on stone metates. They continue to ferment the powerful chicha. And they still bear the Indian countenance — dark eyes with their epicanthic fold, high cheekbones, swarthy complexion, and dark, course hair, all dominant factors in their genes, factors which have survived over five centuries.

But what of their attitudes? Have these changed since Columbus set foot in the New World? Has the acquisition of the transistor radio and the television brought them further into the aura of European civilization and western education? And what contribution to their well-being has their new religion made? Actually it has helped keep the Indian at the very lowest socio-economic level, while at the same time adding to the explosive overpopulation of the Latin American land.

The life of the Aztec was filled with mythology and mysticism, with the priests, the official interpreters of mystic signs, governing the activities of the populace.

The great temples and palaces, the pyramids, the sculpture, the pottery, all the impressive works of art which have been uncovered were representations of their religious belief. The mystique of their religion was left to posterity in written form. Starting in Tenochtitlan through the Yucatan peninsula and Central America, a system of symbolic glyphic writing had developed, unique among the pre-Columbians of the rest of the Western Hemisphere.

With this glyphic writing technique the Aztecs recorded battles and conquests, sacrifices, marriages, births, deaths, taxation and harvests. They used the maguey plant to produce a paper similar to Egyptian papyrus and also wrote on cotton cloth and on cured animal hide writing tablets. The tablets were hinged, folded one into the other, and could be easily stored.

Unfortunately, very little of the Aztec writing remains. The first archbishop of Mexico, Don Juan de Zumarraga, had most of the tablets collected from all parts of Mexico, including Texcuco, the home of the Aztec national archives, piled in the market of Tlatelolco and burned. This terrible travesty was committed because the conquistadores did not understand the strange inscriptions and feared that the beautifully painted manuscripts were magical scrolls which could harm them.

Among the gods of the Aztecs, was the fire-breathing, winged serpent Quetzalcoatl, responsible for the success or failure of crops—indeed a formidable god, although not at the top of their hierarchy. The god at the highest level in their mystic realm was Huitzilopotchli, the god of war, and definitely the supreme deity.

For some unexplained reason, Quetzalcoatl fell out of favor with Huitzilopotchli, and the winged serpent god was exiled from Tenochtitlan (Mexico). On his way he stopped at the city of Cholula, where a temple was later built in his honor. He finally reached the shores of the Gulf of Mexico where he embarked on a sea journey, at which time he was transformed into a tall, fair-skinned man with long hair and beard. It was written that Quetzalcoatl would return in this new form on a definite date in the future, and this belief was perpetuated by the priests.

The Aztec calendar was one of the most precise ever invented, and it was determined by their calendar that Quetzalcoatl would return in the Aztec year which corresponded to 1519 A.D. Coincidentally, it was in the year 1519 that Hernan Cortez, tall, of fair complexion, with long hair and beard, landed on the shores of the Yucatan peninsula.

Moctezuma, the last emperor of the Aztecs, was chosen as their lord because of his qualifications as both a soldier and as a priest. He was selected in preference to his older brothers, one of whom would normally have ascended the throne upon the death of their father. Instead, Moctezuma was chosen, because he had studied for the priesthood and had taken part in many battles. The priests of the Aztecs held great influence over the royalty and the populace. The fact that Moctezuma was a priest as well as the emperor was the predominant factor in the easy defeat of the Aztecs.

Moctezuma firmly believed in the predictions of the priests who perpetuated the legendary tale that Quetzalcoatl would return. When Cortez showed up on the shores of the Yucatan, he was convinced that the prophecy had been fulfilled, that Quetzalcoatl had returned in the same form he took when he was exiled, that Cortez must be his embodiment. Also, many strange events had occurred, beginning in 1510; Lake Tezcuco had overflowed as the result of several big earthquakes, buildings had begun to burn without an apparent reason, and comets to streak through the night sky.

Thousands of Aztecs were slaughtered in battles with the Spaniards, but the ease with which they were killed was not simply because the Spaniards were better soldiers, or that they had firearms. After all, the invaders numbered less than two hundred men against an Indian army of thousands. The Aztecs were trained fighters, notwithstanding the fact that they were equipped with only slings and spears. The Aztec warriors were told by the priests and by Moctezuma himself, that the invader was indeed Quetzalcoatl returned. At first the Aztec defenders hesitated and did not fight offensively, which would have been normal in any other situation, against a different enemy. The Spanish chroniclers of the conquest wrote that in the first battle the Spaniards "had to quit fighting because they had become tired slaying so many Indians, and they could no longer lift their swords above their heads."

The practice of human sacrifice by the Aztecs has always been looked upon as a despicable act, and it was one of the excuses the conquistadores gave for the destruction of the Aztec culture and the forced conversion of the people to Christianity. In fact, the Aztecs did not indiscriminately kill people in their religious ceremonies but instead sacrificed enemy soldiers captured in battle. In doing so, it was believed that they were ennobling the captive, elevating him to a high position after death. It was the Aztec way of displaying respect for those taken prisoner in war (certainly far better than slavery). The captors ate a part of the body of the sacrificed warrior, yet did not consider it to be an act of cannibalism. Instead, it was still one more way in which they could honor and pay respect to their enemy.

The Aztec requirement that the enemy be taken prisoner for later sacrifice was so powerfully motivated that there was a strong effort made during the battles to capture the opponents alive and to avoid killing them on the battlefield. This was especially evident during the conflict with the Spaniards, where numerous Aztec priests were seen throughout the first battles, discouraging the slaying of the Spaniards. The Spanish friars who wrote the accounts of the battles could not comprehend this. They did not understand the strong religious beliefs of the Aztecs, the powerful influence of the priests and the Aztecs' complete obedience to those in command.

The Aztec character and personality can be compared to that of a member of a beehive, where there is no individuality, where all work together for the common good. Although artisans practiced their specialized crafts as potters, goldsmiths, silversmiths, textile weavers, builders and all the skills necessary to the society, there could be no heroes. The cult of individualism did not exist. The farmer was also a soldier and could be called upon at any time to give battle to an enemy. The educated royalty and the priests were the absolute rulers. To question the power of the leader was unthinkable.

The individual with special talent used his skill for the benefit of the entire population. There was no competition within their society.

Much of what we know about the life of the Aztec was written by the Friar Bernal Diaz del Castillo, who sailed with the fleet of Cortez:

> Gazing on such magnificent sights we did not know if they were real, and we were left speechless.... We proceeded along a highway crossing a great lake, a causeway, ten meters wide, from the mainland of the city, which was two miles long,

upon which a multitude of people walked crowded one against the other. There were canoes on the lake, also full of people.... We were met by the king's procession, with the great Moctezuma upon his litter, richly dressed, sitting beneath a canopy of green feathers, and he was beautifully attired in feathers as well as gold and silver and jade. Many in the procession walked before him, sweeping the earth where he might walk and spreading cloths upon it.

We were taken to the great hall where Moctezuma lived and where he provided a meal, which consisted of 300 different plates of food, served by comely young women who brought water to wash the hands of Moctezuma, and then they brought him bread and gave him a drink made from the cacao bean, in a cup of pure gold.

In the palace he (Moctezuma) kept accounts of the revenue, all inscribed in tablets made of a paper, which was called amatl. There was a great warehouse filled with maize and peppers and beans and other storehouses filled with uniforms adorned with gold and precious stones. There were weapons, copper swords, stone knives, bows and arrows and shields and armor made of cotton quilting.

The women were the weavers, working with the cotton and fine feathers...The market place was filled with all sorts of goods, each type having its particular place, foods from all over the kingdom, cloth and sandals, baskets of cacao beans and other vegetables, honey, skins of tigers and lions, fowl and cocks, and young dogs which were bred for food.

The splendid sights which met the Spaniards were almost unbelievable to them. Never had they seen such an abundance of food and artifacts in one place, spread over such a large area. The concept of the central market had not yet occurred to the European. In Europe, trade was carried out as barter with the products carried to the consumer and exchanged for other needed items.

Cortez reported that when his men entered Tlascala, they found "a market place where more than 30,000 people were engaged in buying and selling everything from jewelers' shops filled with gold and silver, and pottery makers displaying their wares, to shops selling food products, and even barber shops and public bath houses." The Aztecs "borrowed" much of their culture, their way of life and artistic style from their predecessors, the Toltecs and from the Maya with whom they traded and whose society can be traced archaeologically back to the year 2000 B.C. The Aztecs, who called themselves Tenochas, founded their capital of Tenochtitlan, (now Mexico City) in the center of a lake in 1325 A.D. In less than 200 years they developed into one of the most powerful civilizations known, conquering an area which encompassed the lower third of North America through most of Central America, including the Yucatan peninsula. When Cortez arrived in Mexico he had no idea of the extent of the Aztec kingdom.

The Aztecs were innovators and fine organizers, cleverly adopting the best from the cultures of their defeated enemies and successfully putting it all to use in their own society. They brought to Mexico from the conquered areas much of the food and other necessities for their growing population, products such as fruits and cacao from the tropics and the luxury items such as gold, copper, jade and precious stones.

But the Aztec conquerors failed to bring the conquered peoples into Aztec society and allowed them to continue to practice their own customs, so that there never developed a loyalty to the Aztec state. Because of this, Cortez was able to recruit the outlying Indian cultures right after he arrived, and several cities joined forces with him against the Aztecs. The Tlaxcalans, hereditary enemies of the Aztecs, supplied Cortez with manpower, food and provisions and accompanied the Spaniards on their way to Tenochtitlan.

When the Spaniards first saw Tenochtitlan, in the valley of what is now Mexico City, they thought they had come to the promised land. On first view, the magnificent landscape of widespread plains, irrigated fields, precisely built roads and the huge pyramids at Teotihuacan astonished and amazed them.

What they saw gave evidence of a superior power and a civilization they least expected. Moctezuma had sent gifts of gold to lay down at the feet of Cortez, and the Spaniards were dazzled by the spoils and the riches of the land.

Recent archaeological excavations have uncovered an Aztec pyramid-temple in the heart of Mexico City — the Templo Mayor, or the Great Temple of the Aztecs, fortunately left intact, surrounded by the government palaces and cathedrals built by the Spaniards, with the labor of the Indians. The Templo Mayor, the beautiful architectural work of the Aztecs, stands revealed today with a staircase cut into its face, reaching over a hundred feet upward to the truncated top of the pyramid, where the sacrificial ceremonies were once practiced. It extends down to a level below the present street surface, surrounded by enormous carved and painted heads of serpents.

Here, today, in the largest city in the world, with a population of over 18,000,000, Indians, Spaniards and meztizos hurry past on their way to government offices, to factories, or to mass, seldom or never thinking about the Aztec who put it all together.

Inheritance

Maria Sanchez was very old, too old to remember her exact age, and was so shrunken and bent, she appeared to be sinking into the ground as she walked, as if seeking a way to enter the earth. Her instinctive, ancient memory, however, was alive. She recalled the time when she was able to quickly and easily skip across this same road from Queretaro, Mexico, leading to the baroque Spanish church. Walking was now an ordeal. She gasped and leaned heavily on a stick, slowly shuffling in her worn sandals over the sun-baked, dusty, stone pavement of the entrance to the church. She remembered a time when tall trees provided shade along the way, but those were long gone.

Her heavily wrinkled, dark Indian face turned upward, and her eyes watered as she looked up at the bright sky, assessing the prospects for today's arrival of tourists. Conditions were good, and she was happy that the heavens were clear and that it probably would not rain. Finally reaching her usual place on the fifth step below the thickly carved and arched wooden doors, she knelt and crossed herself. Then with a deep sigh, she wearily sat down, adjusted her skirts and placed her reed basket beside her. She knew that in this spot a cooling afternoon breeze would soon reach her as it blew across the stone floor of the courtyard outside the church.

Her companions were beginning to arrive. Three of the ancient ones, the usuals, clothed in worn-out, dusty black dresses, heads covered with black shawls. They would all be here today, with their withered, outstretched arms, their pleading eyes and toothless mouths mumbling a hurried blessing to each prospective, passing donor.

She lived alone now in a single room in a tin-roofed shack beside a goat meadow on the outskirts of Queretaro. She was completely abandoned by her children and grandchildren, who had gone to work and live in the city, many miles away. Now this mother, and grandmother, and great grandmother was relegated to begging from tourists and churchgoers for coins to buy the little bit she needed to eke out a living in the remaining days of her life. Nothing more was given in payment for the years of work and hardship.

And all that she could do now was wait for the last day, the final gasp of breath, perhaps here on the steps of the church. She did not despair. She had no conception of who she really was, from whence she came or of her ancestors who had built great civilizations in far better times. She was firmly convinced that glorious days lay ahead, after she was enfolded peacefully in the arms of death.

The world of her ancestors, the pre-Columbians, was not so. There was once monumental achievement, a time of personal fulfillment for the aged, a time of recognition of the old ones, and respect. Respect for the wise old women who had contributed so much to the world — the matriarchs. They governed the families, and this was acknowledged by all, by the populace, by the priests, by the royalty, even by the gods.

Because they had a profound understanding of life based upon their years of experience, and because they could make the important decisions, the women were venerated. Even when they had reached very old age, the matriarchs were counted upon as trusted members of their society.

These same women who in their youth had watched over the hearth, prepared food and chicha, wove textiles, made clothing, and instructed the young ones, were not cast aside when they aged. These old women were the ones called upon to help solve the problems of home and community. They were the matchmakers whose advice was continually sought. The pragmatic, strong and stalwart, the perpetuators of their societies, of their cultures.

The old woman on the fifth step of the church reached out to the tourist couple and received the coin dropped by the young man. He was careful not to touch her hand.

BARRANCOID

The Survivors

BARRANCOID
The Survivors

Venezuela's Orinoco River runs swift, deep and wide, and in some places it is over a half mile across. The current is strong, churning up the bottom and turning the water muddy. Its narrow tributaries, in contrast, are quiet, silver blue, with calm surfaces reflecting the clear sky overhead. These streams, normally filled with large mouth bass and piranhas, become thin and shallow in the dry season, when the river drops and numerous sandbars appear.

In the rainy season, from August through October, the river rises so high it floods many of the small towns along its banks. On its north side lies the town of Barrancas, which means ravines in Spanish, named for the many rivulets which crisscross the area and feed into the Orinoco. Barrancas is not pretty and definitely is not a tourist attraction. It looks the same as most of the towns along the river — untidy. An important cattle distribution center, it has an assortment of small businesses catering mostly to herders and shippers: one 12-room "hotel" which fills to capacity on Friday and Saturday nights, a little restaurant owned by an Italian, a hardware store which does a roaring business in machetes, one pharmacy and the usual two dry goods shops owned by Lebanese who spend most of their days sitting on low stools, hidden from the sun under the shops' awnings, trying to beat one another at backgammon.

The one big difference between Barrancas and the other towns along the river, and an important difference it is to those interested in archaeology, is that from time to time the shops in Barrancas sell authentic, 1000-year-old ceramic pieces. They call these pieces muñecas, meaning dolls, although they bear no resemblance to the dolls little girls play with. Instead, these are the shards and carved figures which once formed part of the burial urns of a very unique group of pre-Columbians, the Barrancoid.

Each year, after the usual torrential rainy season, the river recedes and takes big chunks of earth from along its banks, uncovering the graves of the ancient ones. And each year, when the river is at its lowest, children from surrounding villages climb the banks and dig out the exposed shards of the beautifully worked, brightly glazed urns. Some of the shards slide down the banks to the edges of the river bed, where they are easily retrieved, but if they wash into the main body of water, they are gone forever. The ceramics are quickly carried away and destroyed by the swift action of the current in a relatively short period of time.

It could be said that the children of Barrancas unknowingly assist the science of archaeology by selling the ceramic pieces to local merchants. Not only does this add interest to an otherwise dreary stock of retail goods, but at the same time the children are the unknowing rescuers of pre-Columbian culture, by helping to preserve the ceramics which would be lost to the ravages of the Orinoco.

Upon arrival in dusty, dirty Barrancas, I found it hard to believe that the cosmopolitan capital city of Caracas, with a population of over 3,500,000 and some of the finest hotels, restaurants and residential sections in the world, is only 300 miles north. It is even harder to believe this after some time is spent with the people in the primitive villages which are scattered along the Orinoco's banks. Theirs is a very simple existence. They herd cattle, harvest cotton, take fish from the river, use rope and plank bridges to cross the ravines onto narrow paths leading from one village to the

Shard from a Barrancoid burial urn found in banks of Orinoco by author
Photo: J. Fabry

Shard from a Barrancoid burial urn recovered from Orinoco River
by author
Photo: J. Fabry

Shard from Barrancoid burial urn, Venezuela. Collection of the author

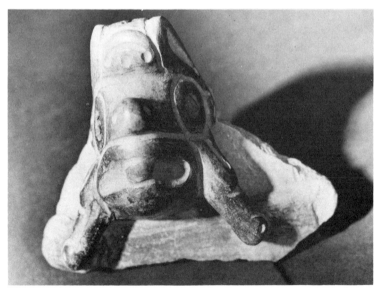

Shard from Barrancoid burial urn, Venezuela. Collection of the author

other. They live in sunbaked clusters of mud-walled, thatch-roofed huts.

On my first visit to Barrancas in 1976, I was accompanied by my good friend and mentor Dave Whitehouse. We were invited into one of the villages to look at some Barrancoid ceramic pieces which had recently been found on the river bank. The earth floors of the huts and the open areas were all packed hard and worn smooth by the bare feet of many generations, and at first glance I could see nothing unusual. I saw many small, and what appeared to be ordinary look- ing white stones scattered just beneath the surface. But a closer look proved that these were not stones, and much to my astonishment, they were bones—human bones! Bones of fingers, vertebrae, ribs, and jawbones with teeth still at- tached, teeth which in places showed through the surface of the compacted earth. I was most impressed by the large amount of children's bones, which could be seen among the others, and upon which the villagers walked as they casually went about their daily lives.

At one point, noticing my fascination with the bones and my attempts to avoid stepping on them, an old women reached down and pried one out of the ground and handed it to me. I thanked her, gave the bone a cursory examina- tion but quickly put it back when she was not looking.

After a couple of hours, I became accustomed to the an- cient human bones beneath my feet, but now, 15 years later, I get an eerie, uncomfortable feeling when I think about the people who live on a pre-Columbian graveyard on the banks of Venezuela's Orinoco.

During this same trip, Dave and I rented a motor-driven hollowed-out log canoe, called a curiare, complete with a boatman, who took us downstream to see some of the small fishing villages. We spent several hours touching shore at many of them, but since it was Saturday nearly everyone had gone upriver to market.

Just as we reached one of the villages, which at first appeared as deserted as the others, a man pulled up in a curiare, hailed us and invited us to come ashore. He was small, dark-skinned, with a pleasant broad welcoming smile and a big black moustache. He told us that his name was Pedro, quickly adding that he was a fisherman, and that he was named after St. Peter, whom he described as "the best fisherman who every lived."

When he learned we were looking for muñecas, he led us to the other side of his hut, pointing to the water's edge. At first I could see nothing. "There are many muñecas to be found in the water," said Pedro, "I saw a few myself yesterday, right over there. Take your shoes off and feel around in the mud with your feet." Although we kept our shoes on we did go into the water up to our ankles and shuffled around, at the same time scooping up mud with our hands. Pedro must have thought we were foolish to go into the water with our shoes on, but he never said a word.

After about a half hour of searching up and down the water's edge, I bumped my shoe against a hard object in the mud. It soon slipped away in the current, and it took a lot of sloshing, sliding and water dancing before I felt it again. This time I was able to hold it with the heel of my shoe and reaching down I scooped up a round, mud covered piece of clay. I hurriedly washed the mud off and a face appeared! A face looked up at me! A monkey's face carved into a six-inch diameter ceramic shard. This had to be part of the decoration of a funeral urn.

We asked Pedro if he knew where the shard had originated or what it represented. He answered, "Señores, this river is full of muñecas this time of the year; clay monkeys, birds, fish and even faces of humans. All my life, as long as I can remember, there have always been muñecas in the river."

We returned to Caracas the next day. I still have the monkey-face shard, and when I take it out of the cabinet to look at from time to time, I remember the trip with Dave, I remember Pedro and the small fishing village on the river, and I wonder how many of these unique ceramic pieces have been lost to the powerful Orinoco during the years since we made that trip. I am glad that at least one Barrancoid monkey shard escaped destruction.

The God of the Orinoco

The bountiful river is our treasure, and we are completely dependent upon her for our existence. While the flow is rough and dangerous, the god of the river is good to us and constant, providing fish to eat and water to nourish the cotton which grows in abundance along the banks. The smaller streams which feed into the river are filled with pavon, the delicious large mouth bass which can be caught in the shallows.

The river bed gives us the clay from which we make the large vessels for the burial of our dead, vessels which assure their safe journey to the other lands. These are fashioned by the special craftsmen who carve the story of the dead into the clay and fire the great urns to provide the good home for those whose breath has gone forever.

When the rains finally depart, the waters retreat and the season of dryness begins. It is then clay can be scooped from the river bed. This is also the season when the small white birds nest in the banks of the river, where we gather the sweet-tasting eggs. The river god brings us everything we need, and her winds assure us that we are never too hot. The gentle winds which blow even during the time of dryness, whisper that soon the rains will come and the river will once again fill and flow with its enormous strength.

My grandfather did not waken to greet the sun this morning, nor shall he ever waken in this world again, for he has gone to meet with our ancestors in the great fishing place. There he will be at peace and very happy as he waits for all of us.

They have fired a great urn for him, decorating it with the glyphs naming the outstanding events of his life, showing what a fine provider he was and also how he was able to communicate with our deceased ancestors. For he was wise indeed —a shaman who could talk to the gods of the rain and river. One of the respected elders, he sat among those who decided the appointment of our leaders. His urn is strong and beautiful. The women have washed his body and dressed him in new garments. Tomorrow we shall carry him to the river bank, where he will be placed inside the urn and buried in the earth.

Burial Customs

The Barrancoid, like all pre-Columbians, were highly concerned with death. They believed that it was necessary to provide the dead with two burials, spaced about a year apart. They probably believed that the spirit of the deceased stayed behind for a certain period of time, and that the spirit would depart when the second burial took place. This ritual of two burials, unique with the Barrancoid, has survived and is still practiced. The Goajiro Indians living in the northwestern part of Venezuela still perform this burial ritual.

The urns used by the Barrancoid for the initial burial were large and very heavy, up to three feet in height, with the clay one-half to three-quarters of an inch thick. They were decorated with many sculptured figures protruding from the surface of the vessels. The heads of a variety of animals, birds, reptiles and fish were so fashioned that they appeared to leap outward from the urns. Turtle heads and monkey faces predominated.

Through their sculpture, the Barrancoid displayed the character and personality of the deceased and also attempted to describe his or her position within the group. Occasionally a shard is found which bears a carved representation of a monkey face with two sets of eyes, one above the other. This is the way the Barrancoid probably indicated second sight, and a shard such as this is most likely from the burial urn of an ancient shaman.

Many of the figures look like gargoyles, with fierce, frightening expressions. All of the anthropomorphic heads appear as though they have protruding tongues, yet these are really representations of a nut or a bean held between the teeth. Despite their grotesque quality, the figures that have been unearthed are artistic and symmetrical. According to experts such as Jose Cruxent, the noted Venezuelan archaeologist, the ceramics are of excellent quality with a high ochre glaze fired onto their smooth surface, retained over 1,000 years' burial in damp earth.

The more decorated the urn, the more important the person buried in it. Importance in the Barrancoid society did not mean that the deceased was rich. In this clan-type chieftainship, material wealth belonged to the entire tribe and was not owned or controlled by the individual. A person's importance within the group was determined by his contributions to the well-being of the society.

The ritual for the dead consisted first in forming and firing the large clay vessel. The body, doubled into a fetal position was placed inside the urn and buried in a shallow grave near the river embankment. They did not build elaborate stone or brick mausoleums, not even if it were the tomb of a chief. The body remained in the earth for a year or more, until decomposed. Then the Barrancoid disinterred the urn, removed the bones, and reburied them in a much smaller, more simply designed vessel, the original large burial urn cast over the cliff, returned to the river where it shattered completely.

The Barrancoid did not build large stone or brick monuments, temples, permanent homes or storage facilities. Their existence did not depend on the harvest of one single crop, and they had no need for food storage in anticipation of a time of shortage. The river provided everything they required and never failed to supply them with food. Climate was good all the year. Their dwellings consisted of small, thatch-roofed, mud-walled huts, easily repaired or replaced. They never had to confront the force of El Niño. The Barrancoid burial urns, which tell us much about the lives of the pre-Columbian inhabitants of Venezuela's Orinoco, show nothing to indicate a warlike people. They did not take slaves, make sacrifices nor express hostility in any way. Quite the contrary. They were peaceful, in tune with their environment, maintaining much respect and admiration for the birds, animals and fish which inhabited their lands and their river.

A highly sensitive and spiritual people, they not only furnished very special care for the body of the deceased, but they also believed that there was a soul which had to be provided for. The double burial ceremony indicates their belief that the soul remained behind until the second burial took place.

At the time of the arrival of the Spaniards no more than 20,000 pre-Columbians lived in the area supported by the Orinoco, and it can be assumed that the Barrancoid had not changed from their original hunter-gatherer way of life. They were not agrarian, did not cultivate fields of corn, had no need to irrigate or terrace the land. They did not build large, permanent stone or adobe brick cities and temples such as those of the sedentary, agrarian societies of Peru.

As can be clearly seen in studying the Chimú, the Moche and the Nazca, or any pre-Columbian agrarian society, it is cultivation and the growth of large populations, the building of great cities, which result in an inability to cope with change. Because of the culture's static structure, it becomes unwieldy and is vulnerable to attack by a superior force.

In the middle of the 16th century, having already settled the city of Caracas, the Spaniards sent a raiding party through the Orinoco region in their never-ending search for gold. They found no gold, nor anything else they considered of value, and so retreated to the northeast, where the armies had already begun the process of wiping out the Caciques, the Indian tribes of Venezuela. The Barrancoid, the Saladoid and the other pre-Columbians of the Orinoco fled to the northwest and so avoided the Spanish onslaught which no doubt would have wiped them out completely.

They were able to travel easily, accustomed to living off the land, and it was no great hardship for them to gather a few belongings and move to another place. The homes they left behind were simple mud and thatch structures and could easily be rebuilt elsewhere in a day or two. If necessary they could sleep under the stars on a reed hammock stretched between two trees.

In this manner the pre-Columbian Indians of the Orinoco were able to survive, moving out quickly to avoid the Spaniards. Simply and easily, with few complications, they found a new land to the north and west where they took on a different way of life and became the Goajiro.

There is ample evidence to prove that besides Venezuela, the Barrancoid inhabited parts of the West Indies. In 1970, archaeologists in Puerto Rico uncovered several ceramic shards from beneath the wall of a 16th-century cathedral in the harbor of San Juan. These pieces, parts of burial urns, representing monkey faces, birds, turtles and anthropomorphic figures are almost exact duplicates of finds from the Barrancoid culture on the banks of the Orinoco in Venezuela. They must have first sailed to nearby Trinidad and Tobago, then northward, from island to island until they reached Puerto Rico.

The Goajiro

Books on sociology or anthropology give scant attention to the Goajiro Indians, perhaps because these people did not call attention to themselves. It is known that the Ciboney and Arawak populated the Caribbean and that they were later replaced by the fierce Carib who set the stage for the arrival of the Spaniards. While the movement and intermingling of these different groups was in progress throughout the West Indies, the Goajiro established their culture in what is now the Goajiro Peninsula on the northern plains of Venezuela west of Lake Maracaibo.

The Goajiros are a xenophobic people, who have always kept to themselves and never adopted European ways. They herded cattle and tended goats. Cows were unknown in the Americas before the 15th century when they were brought from Europe in the ships of Columbus. Cattle became a means of survival for the displaced pre-Columbians of the Orinoco. They became nomadic herdsmen, following the seasonal supply of water. Although the Goajiro do not purchase fancy cars and do not live in modern dwellings, they are people of considerable means. They might even be called rich, deriving their wealth from cattle herding. Their money cannot be counted since it never gets to a bank. Instead they convert it to gold which they bury in secret places.

While the exact census is unknown, since they do not register births and deaths and do not carry identification papers, it is estimated that the Goajiro number around 150,000, therefore considered to be a "successful" society. In sociological terminology a successful society is one which has experienced an increase in population, as opposed to an unsuccessful society whose numbers have declined.

Besides the everyday occupation of cattle herding, the men fish and hunt, while the women do most of the basic household work, the food preparation and child rearing. The Goajiro have their own language, their own manner of dress, their own religion and their own customs. They borrow nothing from the few outsiders with whom they have contact. The society is fundamentally matriarchal, the women making most of the important decisions. The men are respected as fine archery craftsmen and good shots.

The different Goajiro tribes have distinctive identifying symbols, the frog, turtle, lizard, jaguar and bird; these are branded on their livestock, frequently displayed on their gold jewelry, and even tattooed on their women. These same animal and bird symbols are found on the burial urns of the Barrancoid.

They produce colorful, woven wool rugs and shawl-like printed cotton dresses, called mantas, items which are much sought after by tourists. They make necklaces of tuma stones, highly polished pink semiprecious stones, which have great value among them and which are passed on to their daughters. These beautiful necklaces hardly ever fall into the hands of outsiders. The tumas are sometimes buried in the grave of a Goajiro woman.

Whites are not allowed to witness the burial of a Goajiro, but it is known that they have a double burial ritual, a carry-over from their Barrancoid ancestors. The body is disinterred after a year or more, the bones thoroughly cleaned by the women of the immediate family, and after an elaborate ceremony are permanently reburied in a small ceramic vessel. Since the Goajiro cemeteries are well hidden and the sites not charted, neither looters nor archaeologists have ever found an original burial urn.

The Goajiro matriarchal system is evident in their dance, during which the women with painted faces, dressed in voluminous mantas, use embracing and aggressive gestures towards the men who dance naked except for headband and loincloth. The dance is performed by one couple at a time, encircled by the other dancing couples, taking turns in the center, to a constant fast drum beat.

The Goajiros are prosperous, self-sufficient, and in control of their surroundings. They are independent, free spirits. They are survivors.

CHIMÚ
The City Builders

THE CHIMÚ
The City of Chan-Chan

Around 1000 B.C. on the northwestern coastal desert of Peru, a group of people established a society which evolved into one of the most sophisticated of all South American pre-Columbian cultures. They were the Chimú, the founders of the empire of Chimor, builders of a complex, agricultural state with a strong governmental system where control was maintained through a hierarchy of rulers, priests, administrators and tax collectors. It would seem that they were invincible and could cope with any circumstance which might cause a change in their environment. However, this was not the case. After establishing a whole new system, after developing an amazing, multifaceted civilization, the Chimú completely disappeared.

Why did this happen? How did they vanish so suddenly? What catastrophic event caused an empire of several million people to dissolve into nothing? During the expansion of the empire of Chimor, other pre-Columbian societies were developing in different parts of Peru, all of which were eventually conquered by the Inca. Some archaeologists consider the Chimú one of those, but it cannot be said that the Chimú as a society really existed at the time of the expansion of the Inca. The Chimú culture had been destroyed, their cities turned to shambles and their lands into a state of ruin long before the Inca advanced.

I wanted to see for myself. To see the remains of an important culture, and to learn all I could about what had happened to an ancient civilization.

On the flight from Lima, the approach to the airport of Trujillo took us over the ancient walled city of Chan-Chan, which from the air appears as though it were the immense foundation for a gigantic, abandoned modern building project in the middle of the desert. On the road to town I once again passed the labyrinth of Chan-Chan, and that time I saw it from taxicab level. Close up, it looks as if those miles and miles of giant walls were made of enormous milk chocolate rectangles left to melt under a hot sun.

Chan-Chan, built entirely of adobe brick, covering an area of eight square miles, consists of ten rectangular-shaped, walled dwelling complexes, called ciudadelas, or small towns. At the height of the empire of Chimor, around 800-1000 A.D., these ciudadelas were precisely built, architecturally perfect structures, with trapezoidal, frieze-covered walls, decorated with brightly painted, low-relief designs. Most of the walls were completely covered with geometric figures, stylized designs of birds, fish, reptiles, shells, as well as anthropomorphic and human shapes. The pelican at rest is an often-repeated motif.

The 20-foot high walls are 10-to-12 feet wide at their bases, and graduate to three feet in width at the top. Most of them are stone reinforced at the bottom, protecting the walls for over 1000 years, through dozens of earthquakes.

Today, worn down by wind, storm, flood and tectonic activity, Chan-Chan remains a roofless maze of walkways, ramps, burial platforms and audiencias. These audiencias, or hearing chambers, were the parliaments of the Chimú, where petitions of the populace were heard by the rulers and priests. They are enclosed, 2,000-square-foot, rectangular patios, with several niches built into the walls, where the judges sat. They are so acoustically perfect that a normal speaking voice coming from one of the niches can be accurately heard over the entire patio.

Each ciudadela had two ceremonial halls, one large hall for the populace and a smaller one for the use of royalty. The ciudadelas contained large water reservoirs, 450 X 150 feet, and 20 feet deep, fed by underground springs. All the enclosures were designed with one entrance and only a single, narrow pathway leading to it, requiring pedestrians to approach in single file. These enclosures divided the segments of their society, separating royalty from the populace. The walls were built so high, scaling them would have been impossible, and since the people could not enter the narrow doors except one by one, complete control of traffic was maintained.

A series of ramps led to burial platforms housing the tombs of rulers. Llamas were sometimes buried with them to assure a food supply on the journey to the next world. The wives of the rulers were usually buried beside them.

Chan-Chan at the height of its development, around 500 A.D., was the largest city in the world with a population of at least 100,000. It was hundreds of years later that the capitals of Europe, Asia and Africa numbered as many people. A walk through the remains of Chan-Chan can be compared to walking through a maze, since the walls were laid out in such a confusing manner. It was difficult to weave our way through without getting lost, retracing our steps, changing our course, and sometimes going around in circles. The walls of the ciudadelas still standing are not nearly as tall as they were before El Niño wreaked its destruction, and in some places I was able to see over the tops, which should have made it easier for me to know in which direction I was going, but it didn't! How much more confusing it must have been when the walls were at their full height. Why were they built this way? Was this a ploy of

Restored Wall, Chan-Chan, Peru

Chan-Chan

Huaca Esmeralda (Pyramid of the Emeralds) Trujillo, Peru

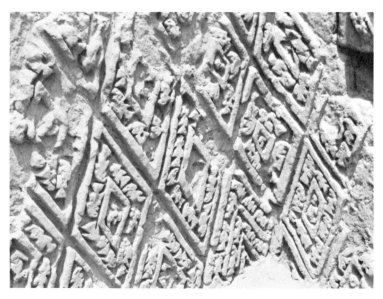

Frieze detail, Chan-Chan, Peru

Chan-Chan

Chan-Chan

Burial platform, Chan-Chan

Restored Wall, Chan-Chan

Audiencia (hearing chamber), Chan-Chan

Chan-Chan

The author in Chan-Chan

Trapezoidal wall, Chan-Chan

Chan-Chan

Maize storage chambers, Chan-Chan

Chan-Chan

Chan-Chan

Huaca del Sol (Pyramid of the Sun), Trujillo, Peru

Large ceremonial plaza, Chan-Chan

Nazca ceramic, courtesy Museum of Archaeology and Anthropology, Lima.

the priests to baffle the common people and keep them away from the palaces of the rulers, or was this done to perplex an enemy in case of an attack upon the city? Perhaps both reasons are correct.

A close look at Chan-Chan reveals that the Chimú had a stratified society in which the larger part of the population was obligated to furnish the labor and a higher-ranking class to consume and thereby afford opportunities for labor to produce. Production was balanced by consumption with the balance maintained by an elaborate bureaucracy. The royalty was also responsible for the storage and distribution of goods and the collection of taxes. Storage of food products was the backbone of the system and population growth was related to the amount of food on hand. As the population grew, more food was needed to be stored, and the product most suited for storage was corn.

Elaborate burials in the royal tombs also provided for a continuous disposal of stored products. These burials plus the need to support the military force, frequent celebrations, marriages, travel by the nobility and sacrificial burnings, all were activities which systematically consumed goods.

There is not sufficient evidence to determine whether or not the Chimú had a caste system, but it is quite certain that their society was rigid and static. The architecture of Chan-Chan, showing a strong concern for social control, points to a bifurcated system. The extremely high walls, the maze-like corridors, the single entry, all indicate that there was a desire to separate the populace from the nobility.

An anonymous history of Trujillo written by Spaniards in the 16th century, tells that the founder of Chimor was Toycanamo who had nine successors. Toycanamo was a mythical figure, supposed to have come out of the sea. The last ruler was Minchancaman who was king up to 1470, when he was defeated by the rising Inca empire.

Each major compound, or ciudadela, was built by a different ruler, to house himself, his seat of government, and to serve as a center for the management of his wealth. The Chimú royalty obeyed the law of split inheritance, whereupon the king's death, his palace passed on to a corporation of secondary heirs, while the principal heir became the next king of Chimor, who then built a new palace and compound.

The Pacific Reed Boat Theory

A legend persists that the ancestors of the Chimú came in reed boats and landed on the northwest coast of Peru where they found the fishing good and the weather favorable. Here, the Humboldt current carried the cool waters up from the southern Pacific and with it an abundance of life from the sea. Peru's coastline, whose waters are highly charged with nutrients, is one of the richest in the world. To the Chimú, this was an idyllic place to make a home.

While the Chimú men fished rich harvests from the sea, the women gathered wild fruits, roots and tubers from the land. It was probably during one day of gathering that they came upon shoots of wild corn, whose seed had been born on the wind from some distant place, or carried in the guano of a bird and dropped to the ground where it germinated. The Chimú soon learned that they could easily plant the kernels which would take root quickly to become tall stalks bearing many ears of fine, yellow maize.

This simple cereal was the find of all finds. A discovery which was the single most important event in the epoch of the pre-Columbian Indians, and the turning point in the life of the much-travelled hunter-gatherers. They could now remain in one place and build a permanent home, since they no longer needed to follow the wandering herds for sustenance. With little effort, and in a short time, a fine crop of maize could be cultivated, and all that was required was sun and water and some dried seed kernels. The wonderfully cool, fresh waters running down from the melting snows of the Andes provided continuous irrigation.

Before the great discovery it was necessary to fish on a daily basis, no matter what the conditions of the seas. They fished most of the day to provide food for one or two meals, since the catch had to be consumed rapidly to avoid spoilage. Also, fishing was dangerous work. Many were drowned with sudden changes in weather, when a strong wind could easily capsize the caballitos de tutumo, little horses made of reeds, the name given to the fishing boats, still in use all along the coast of Peru.

Maize Brings Civilization

With the cultivation of large crops of marvelous maize, enough to feed everyone, fishing became the supplementary part of their diet, and they found that now there was leisure time, time to rest while the corn grew, time to dream and to create, time to build the cities and temples, time to fire the storytelling clay vessels which were buried with the dead, time to weave the colorful mantles of cotton and wool.

With only 80 to 90 days of labor in the fields and on the terraces, a family of five could produce enough corn to provide themselves and their farm animals with the bulk of their food requirements for an entire year. Their lives now became relegated to the needs of the crop, and the center of all their attention turned to corn. Just as in their past the hunt had been the most important of all events, so the planting and harvesting of maize became to the Chimú the very purpose for their existence.

And as their numbers grew, they became more and more tied to the land, remaining in one place, cultivating the crops which had to sustain an ever-increasing population. The Chimú, who were once a simple group of hunter-gatherers following the herd, became a complex agricultural society, the vast empire of Chimor.

Grave Goods

Ceramic pottery, silver ornaments and woven textiles buried in the tombs of the Chimú were preserved over the centuries because of the extremely dry atmosphere in the desert region of northern Peru. A large number of ceramic vessels were designed with the sculptured figures of rulers, priests, soldiers, farmers, fishermen, artisans and builders of cities and temples. While these ceramic portraits provide a detailed look at the routine lives of the Chimú, there is another group of unique vessels which merit special attention and have a unique story to tell, the whistling pots of Chimor.

Music was an important part of the life of the Chimú, and they invented many instruments, which were used for both ritual and pleasure, mostly wind instruments, such as flutes and ocarinas, made of clay or copper. Many instruments have been found in the tombs, and must have been used in the burial ceremony, as musical accompaniment to funeral processions. Among these are the intriguing whistling pots, and they are something very special.

These highly glazed, black, (carbon application before firing produced the black glaze) double bowl vessels were some of the most complicated of all pre-Columbian ceramics. They were made with a strirrup-like handle connecting two bowls, so that they could be easily held, and with a tube-like opening at the top, where water was poured to fill the vessels beneath. The two-section bowl was usually designed in the shape of a seabird with the head and beak forming the spout. If it is half-filled, and swayed from end to end, the sloshing of the water drives air into the head, where it is forced into a stream and split into sound-producing vortexes. The wind, the sea and the whistling of birds were clearly reproduced. Varying the amount of water in the pot changed the pitch.

The Inca borrowed the unusually versatile whistling pot concept from the Chimú and played it as a wind instrument, half filling it with water and blowing directly through the opening. Recent studies of the whistling pots of the Inca and Chimú have determined that these intricately constructed instruments produce pure musical notes. Thousands have been examined by experts who have learned that they are all acoustically different, yet they harmonize one with the other if they come from the same cultural group.

Music, a true measure of cultural complexity, is still another proof of the highly advanced civilizations which existed along the Peruvian coastal desert. Today, the Indians of Peru use the quena, a bamboo flute which produces a round, soulful sound. The quena, an instrument far simpler than those made by the Chimú, is played by descendants of the Inca, the Quechua-speaking people of the Andes.

The empire was at its height around 1000 A.D. and dominated until the arrival of the Inca. The remains of Chimú cities, their road system, irrigation canals, pottery and textile design, demonstrate that they were people of accomplishment. They converted an inhospitable desert into a productive land and provided abundant harvests for a population of over 3,000,000.

They lived an agrarian existence, and while appearing to have been mostly concerned with their fields and crops, normally serene and peaceful endeavors, the Chimú were in effect warlike. It was through conquest that they extended their realm for over a thousand miles along the Peruvian coastline and west beyond the Andes. The people defeated in battle were either taken as slaves or killed in sacrificial ceremonies. Many of the former enemies possessing specific talents were absorbed into Chimú society to become the artisans and builders of roads, irrigation canals, palaces and temples.

An intricate system of roadways was built for the transportation of goods throughout the empire. Good roads were needed for use by the military and for the collection of the mit'a, the corn labor tax imposed upon the populace. Waystations were maintained at strategic points where adobe brick warehouses were built to store the corn. Periodically, the government tax collectors would travel those highways and collect the revenue from the widespread farming populace, not easily accomplished in an empire extending over such large distances, which only could be travelled on foot, for like the Maya and the other pre-Columbian societies, the Chimú had no carts, no domesticated beasts of burden and made no use of the wheel. Though the Chimú may have used the sea at times, sailing in rough waters was precarious in small fishing boats which could easily capsize. The ocean on the western coast of South America is not as pacific as its name implies.

Wherever the wheel exists and roads are built over hills or mountains, they are sure to wind upward and downward, curving so that the elevations are reached gradually, making the ascent easier for a wheeled vehicle pulled by a person or a draft animal. However, exploration of the roads built by the pre-Columbians shows that they were constructed straight up and down the inclines, without curving. While it may be the shortest distance, for an animal pulling a cart up the side of a mountain it is far easier on a winding road than on one which has a direct ascent. This perpendicular construction indicates that the roads were designed for people only and not for draft animals pulling wheeled carts.

Since all travel was pedestrian, goods had to be transported on the backs of people, or tied to a bundle on the end of a pole and dragged along the ground. The llama, called "the camel of the Andes," did not come into widespread use until the time of the Inca. The Chimú did raise llamas, but they were used only for food. The llama was not a very efficient beast of burden. If more than 40 pounds were placed on its back, or a person tried mounting one, it would stop, remain fixed to the ground and would not take a step forward. It is not unusual today to see a farmer in Cuzco walking up a hillside with over 100 pounds on his back, leading two or three lightly burdened llamas, with ribbons in their ears, trotting daintily alongside.

The concept of the wheel never occurred to the pre-

Columbian. Their pottery was not turned. Instead, they used the coil method, whereby clay was rolled into ropelike lengths, placed in graduated circles, one above the other and smoothed by pinching and drawing out, with the hands used as paddles.

The potters and metal workers were kept on the outskirts of the settlements, where the kilns could be fired safely. Huge piles of broken shards found today, represent areas of pottery making, and the shards are not just the results of exposure to the elements. Instead, these are quantities of ceramics which did not come up to standard in firing. If a piece did not meet expectations, it was cast out of the pottery workshop and wound up on the discard heap. The piles of unwanted shards, yesterday's refuse, are today's archaeological treasures.

Most of the ceramic pieces, especially those which were highly glazed and decorated, were used for religious purposes. Vessels were filled with food and buried in the graves, the finer ceramic pottery not used for cooking or for storage of food. Natural gourds were used for eating and drinking.

The priests taught the technique of pottery-making, directing its design and production. They presented the people with pieces of fine pottery as rewards for good work and gave them to the military for success in battle. Ceramics were regarded with reverence and respect, much the same as medals are in society today, and the presentation of ceramics was one of the means by which the priesthood maintained control over the populace. Ceramic pottery was a communication device, a way of expressing religious feeling, an object of worship and a symbol of achievement.

Canal Builders

Irrigation was a critical factor in the Chimú's agricultural system. They had to bring the necessary water from rivers fed by mountain streams 50 to 60 miles away, and the well-engineered canals they built to do this remain a testament to their skills. The canals were dug with such precision, they serve today as examples of good hydraulic construction. Engineers studying the Chimú irrigation system believe they used a clay bowl-and-water-level surveying device for calculating the heights and angles in laying out the routes of the canals. In some places the force of the water was controlled by placing large rocks on the floors of the canals, to prevent the erosion of the walls, and there is a calculated variance in the widths and depths, to prevent the waters from rushing and to maintain a steady flow.

La Cumbre is the longest and most impressive of all the canals built, running 50 miles from the north in Chicama, south to the Moche Valley, not far from the capital city of Chan-Chan. More work went into the planning and preparation of this canal, so vital to their irrigation system, than into any other hydraulic project, yet it was never used. They started to build this canal right after the first big flood caused by El Niño at the beginning of the 12th century, when massive uplifting of the land along the coast occurred and resulted in diminished supplies of water from the north.

Large quantities of soil and gravel had to be transported from the valley below to the tops of the slopes where the canal was laid out. The excavation for the canal can still be seen, twisting and turning through the mountains, and remains as yet another monument to the ingenuity of those pre-Columbians, who no doubt were forced to abandon the project because of the extreme tectonic activity along the coast at that time.

Nevertheless, thousands of canals were put into use, carrying precious water to the terraced slopes and to the valleys below, turning the desert into a vast, productive agricultural system. Terracing the slopes made it possible to take advantage of increased land surface for cultivation and at the same time control irrigation.

Tortilla y chicha

He awakened early to the rhythmic, staccato, slapping sounds his wife's hands made as she shaped the dough for the corn bread, their first food of the day. The sounds stopped from time to time when a sufficient quantity was ready for the oven. His hunger was intensified by the aroma of baking corn bread which drifted into their hut from the adobe hearth outside, and he hoped there would be some bread left over to take to the fields for a midday meal. The two sons working with him would no doubt ask for more than was available, and today would be particularly trying and long, with the preparation of the terraces for next season's crop of corn.

His tooth began to throb, and he thought if the pain grew, he would go to the temple and obtain a soothing herb from one of the priests.

As his wife walked by, his thoughts shifted to her swelling abdomen. Would it not be wonderful, if the next child were a girl selected to live in the temple, to be taught by the priests in the ways of the sun-god. How greatly hon-

ored is the father of such a girl! Perhaps this was too much to ask, and yet, while he was at the temple, he would make a small offering.

His wife's mother began to prepare the chicha, the corn mash made into a delightful beer. An intermittent splashing sounded from time to time as she spewed some of the mash from her mouth into the vessel to start the fermentation. The chicha would be ready in one week's time, ready for the festival of the rebirth of the sun in the heavens.

His tooth began to ache again. Yes, he would go to the temple, perhaps tomorrow.

"The People"

The Chimú had no doubt that theirs was the strongest of all kingdoms, one that would remain so for a long, long time. They were "the people" and as such the very best on earth, undefeated in battle, indefatigable in their efforts to expand the empire. Besides, didn't they have the gods on their side? Wasn't their lord the sun-god himself, and wouldn't he always protect them and care for their needs? It would have been difficult for them to imagine that anything could happen to change the normal course of things in such a rich and powerful society.

Unfortunately, the Chimú were wrong, and as the result of a completely unexpected series of natural catastrophes, the collapse of the system took place, eventually causing the complete disappearance of their culture.

What happened is not exactly known, since most of the destruction was caused by force of nature. The findings of archaeologists, geologists and anthropologists are nebulous and a good deal of conjecture has to be employed because most of the evidence is in fragments, and the Chimú left no written record of those cataclysmic times.

Anthropology has provided one definite clue. The skeletal remains of the Chimú show a considerable amount of pitting of the bone on the lower back portion of the skull, a medically acknowledged sign of extreme malnutrition. If the Chimú experienced hunger to such an extent, it could only mean that there had been a failure of their most important food source, corn, and if the corn crop had failed, it could have happened only because those well-engineered irrigation systems also had failed.

El Niño

The name "El Niño" was used by the Spanish-speaking people of Latin America for hurricane. Translated literally El Niño means "The Child." The name has another meaning however, since it also refers to the Christ child, whose spirit is said to return each year at Christmas. This same name was also given to the periodic, catastrophic, climatic changes which take place along the Pacific coast of South America every seven to ten years. The Humboldt current, which runs northward along this coast, brings with it a constant flow of cool water and abundant sea life from the Antarctic waters. Underneath this flow, on the ocean floor, is a fault, which is part of a series of prolonged tectonic activity.

From geological evidence, El Niño has been returning periodically for the past several thousand years, probably as far back as the last Ice Age. The recent volcanic eruptions of Mount St.Helens, followed by several major California earthquakes, show that El Niño has reached far up the side of North America as well.

From all indications, El Niño made its appearance at the height of the Empire of Chimor, when there was a strong movement of the earth's crust along the coast, causing an upward thrust of 60 feet or more in that precise area. This resulted in extensive flooding which severely damaged the coastline and at the same time devastated the canals and irrigation systems of the Chimú. Without sufficient supply of water, far less farmland could be irrigated, and the corn crop failed. Evidently there was not enough time to rebuild the system, since a whole series of major earthquakes took place over an extended period. Also, the warming of the waters of the Humboldt current caused destruction of sea life, and the normal catches were severely diminished.

Around 1400 A.D. a Niño of such catastrophic scope weakened the empire that it never recovered. The canals were damaged, abandoned, and never rebuilt. The attempted repairs were not enough to enable the Chimú to regain full strength. The empire was destroyed by the raw power of nature, and the Chimú lost the battle for survival.

Had these same events taken place in 500 B.C., and they very well might have considering the geological activity of the region, the lives of the Chimú would undoubtedly have been altered, but they would not have been completely destroyed. If these events took place 2,000 years earlier, when the Chimú were living a nomadic existence, they were equipped to travel quickly from one place to the other. The hunter-gatherers would have survived.

It is my theory that what caused the destruction was the system based exclusively upon agriculture, which was the only possible way of feeding such a large, sedentary population. The system fell apart because of specialization, and the division of labor reduced the individual's capacity for survival.

They no longer possessed the capability of gathering up family and weapons and starting on the long trek in search of the herd. They had actually forgotten how to hunt and live off the land. They were too dependent upon the rulers and the priests. Their population was too large and they had become too unwieldy. They lost flexibility and maneuverability. They had become too civilized.

Their deep religious belief contributed to their destruction. After all, wouldn't the gods always provide for those who built the temples and made the offerings? Wasn't their own king a living god? Wasn't maize the food of the gods and wouldn't it last forever?

It did not last forever. The crops failed, the system failed and the Chimú came to an end. The remaining few scattered along the coast of Peru were eventually assimilated into the Inca empire or killed off. Spanish historians claim that the Chimú were conquered by the Inca, but this is not true, because at the time of the emergence of the Inca, around 1200 A.D., the Chimú as a culture no longer existed.

Premonitions

I dreamed confusing dreams last night, reliving our attack upon the Chavin to the north. Although they were brave fighters, we took many heads and brought back a large number of captives to Chan-Chan. I dreamed that my father, the sun-god, was so pleased that he presented me with four beautiful girls of the court as wives, and allowed the sacrifice of six captives as a celebration of this important event. We must plan to return to the land of the Chavin, for there are still many riches to be taken.

Today I shall be dressed in the splendor of many colored feathers, for it is the day of the Inti-Raymi, the summer solstice, the day the sun rides longest in the heavens, and we shall go to the great plaza to welcome the sun, to sing and pray to him. The people shall look well upon me, for I am to be the next sun-god. The priests will surely order special figures to be cast and vessels to be fired in commemoration of this day.

I recall my dream of last night and what it was that disturbed me. I dreamed it was during our journey north to give battle to the Chavin. We had stopped at some of the way stations to replenish our supplies, and to our dismay, there was little corn in the warehouses which at this time of the year should be full. This perplexed and concerned me. I shall have to talk to those responsible. Perhaps I shall have a word with the tax collectors.

I must think about this after the Inti-Raymi solstice, for my slaves have now come to dress me for the great day.

RIDDLE

Are there lessons to be learned from the story of the Chimú? Is there a natural sequence of events which always takes place and which is unavoidable in complex, agrarian societies?

Large scale agriculture demanded a sedentary existence. As the crops grew, so the population expanded. A larger and larger work force was continually in demand for producing larger crops, and necessitating the need for a division of labor. Organized religion was required to appease the gods. The construction of great cities and temples, the ues were all necessary to supplicate the supernatural beings to bring the sun and water to the land. There was also the need to evoke the god's protection in an afterlife, the demand for military conquest to obtain more and more land — to continue the endless cycle until inevitable destruction.

The culture leaves behind the wonderful products of its creativity, works of art, the tangible evidence of a strong religious belief, but the culture itself disappears. It falls apart because of an inherent weakness in the system, which causes it to disintegrate in the face of adversity. In the case of the Chimú, their downfall was brought about by a natural disaster from which they could not recover.

Before their culture became so complex, and while they were still the hunter-gatherers, every member of the clan knew how to protect his life and the lives of those close to him. At an early age each male learned to fashion weapons for the hunt, how to stalk and bring down the prey and how to find or construct a shelter. They could move quickly and easily from one place to the other. They followed the herd, and they were never tied down to the land. The clan was not allowed to grow too large, because the hunt provided only a limited amount of food. They always retained the ability to adjust to environmental change. After all, they were the hunters, those who had to constantly pit their skill and stamina against wild animals. Didn't their very lives depend upon quick adjustments, fast movements and rapid responses?

After they became sedentary cultivators of crops, the Chimú lost this adaptability to environmental change, and when they needed to move on and drastically alter their way of life, they could not do so. Specialization had taken its toll, and they could no longer return to their former hunter-gatherer existence. They had forgotten how to track down the herd, forgotten how to hunt, and so they starved to death. The few who remained were easily conquered and assimilated by the Inca. The Chimú culture disappeared.

What is left of their great civilization? Pitiful remains of empty-shell cities, whose walls look as if they had gone through an intensive bombing: washed-out roads, destroyed terraces and canals, shards of pottery, broken clay figures and shreds of woven textiles left behind, together with the skeletons of the dead, forsaken on a Peruvian desert.

MOCHE

The Warriors

MOCHE
Lima, Peru – 1991

In September of 1991 I returned to Peru to complete the research I needed for this book. Friends and relatives advised me not to go because of the newspaper reports of terrorism, social unrest and political turmoil in that country. Regardless of the well-meant advice, and after much deliberation, I decided to make the trip. I am so glad I did, because otherwise this would not have been written.

It was strange to think that I was probably the only one on the flight to Lima who was not a Peruvian or a foreign businessman. The last time I was on an airplane going to Lima was 1976, and most of the passengers were tourists. Peruvians couldn't afford the trip then, but times have changed, and some of them now have plenty of dollars to spend. Upon arrival at the baggage claim area, I saw that boxes far outnumbered suitcases, and the cartons taken off our flight from Miami contained mostly large screen televisions, personal computers and microwave ovens.

The capital had changed a great deal during the past fifteen years, from a city that was once a treasure for tourists, to one which has become dismal and dangerous. The museums were still filled with wonderful Peruvian archaeological artifacts, and the people were as charming and solicitous as they always were. However, it was difficult to ignore the presence of armed guards everywhere, and army squads patrolling airports with walkie-talkies and attack dogs. I felt the ever pervasive fear that stalks the city.

I felt this fear all the time I was in Lima. The Sendero Luminoso (Shining Path) terrorists, trying to discredit the legitimate government with bombings, shootings and kidnappings, were the reason for my trepidation. They were also the cause of much disruption and pain for the stoic people of Peru. During my stay in Lima several students were killed, and a 26-hour blackout resulted from the bombing of two main power stations, all the work of the Sendero Luminoso. Power shortages were a way of life and expected at any time of day or night. Most retail businesses had gasoline generators which shopkeepers placed just outside the doors when the power failed. The blasting noise of the generators sounded as if trip-hammers were breaking the concrete sidewalks on all the streets of Lima.

Thousands of taxis, mostly old Volkswagens, sped through the city streets, driven by polite and fairly well-educated men, who for the most part held down another job besides that of driving a cab. There were political philosophers among them. I asked one what he thought of the Sendero Luminoso, and he answered, " How can Marxism succeed in Peru when it failed after 75 years in a country as large Russia? No, the terrorists will eventually be wiped out."

The shops selling alpaca rugs, gilded mirrors and Indian artifacts had moved from the center of the city to the outskirts where the rent was cheaper. The expensive locations on the streets off the main plazas in the center of the city were occupied by retailers of cassette players and records, television sets and computers.

The new, heavily guarded enclosed shopping malls in the suburban areas were filled with boutiques which carried imported clothing, cameras, watches and jewelry. The many travel agencies sold mostly round-trip airline tickets to Miami. Pizzerias had replaced the old Peruvian seafood restaurants.

Money changers were everywhere. At any time of the day and late into the night, dozens of persuasive young men could be seen doing business at every major intersection and street corner, carrying neatly arranged stacks of $100 bills in one hand and Peruvian *sols* in the other. One million *sols* was the equivalent of $1.00 until I arrived, at which time the government struck off all the zeros. Instant deflation! The money changers operated right under the noses of the local police, who completely ignored this illegal activity. There probably was more U.S. currency on the streets of Lima than in most American cities. All the dollars came from major traffic in coca leaves, from which a basic paste material was made in Peru and shipped to the "laboratories" in Colombia for the production of cocaine.

Clandestine army death teams had begun operating, not against the coca dealers, but to wipe out suspected Sendero Luminoso members. In October 1991, a late-night attack killed 16 people. It was learned the next day that they mistakenly "hit" the wrong house and that innocent citizens had been murdered.

This was not the Lima I knew. From the moment I arrived in the city, until I left, I did not see anyone on the streets with a smiling, happy face. Grimness and worried looks were everywhere. Nobody walked slowly. People moved quickly from place to place, with suspicion, mistrust and furtiveness in their eyes.

The museums of Lima were my refuge. I spent most of the time renewing my acquaintance with these institutions which had fortunately preserved the wonderful artifacts of Peruvian pre-Columbian history. The museum directors, the archaeologists, the guides, opened their doors to me. All were most helpful. I was given permission to photograph the exhibits and visit the workshops where newly-arrived, recently uncovered pieces were being studied and assembled for display. There, in the museums I felt safe. There, was trust and certainty.

Groups of high school students arrived daily, under the tutelage of their professors who conducted toured lectures through the exhibits. These young Peruvians learned about their ancestors. Their faces showed pride and belongingness. They were an essential part of something important. It was not just knowledge these student sought, it was the connection to their heritage, to something real and meaningful. For them it was also an escape from the depravity of the world outside.

As I left the museum on my last evening in Lima, I thought there might still be hope for the country, but my thoughts were quickly shattered by a blackout over the city, the blasting noise of sirens, and soldiers standing with rifles at all the main intersections.

I was glad to leave Lima the next morning for the trip to Trujillo, and to enter the Moche and Chimú country, 300 miles to the north.

Complex of the Witch

It was with some apprehension that I got on the bus in the early-morning, busy, market plaza of Trujillo to take the 65-mile trip north to Cartavio, a town which did not even appear on any of my maps. I didn't know what to expect. Very small Cartavio sits in the center of large, important sugar cane fields, and the bus which had only 30 passenger seats, was full of people going there for the start of the harvesting season. So it was standing room only during the shaky, two-hour trip on the Pan American highway. This is one of the worst, pot-holed roads I have ever travelled. On one bad curve, a standing passenger landed in my lap with a basket containing two tied-up, squawking, live turkeys. Accompanying the groaning motor was the blasting sound of a relentless transistor radio strapped to the dashboard, directly in front of the driver. From time to time he added to the noise by singing to the music in a loud, raucous voice.

It was a relief to get off the bus and step down into the sudden, welcome quiet of Cartavio's town square. There was only one taxi waiting, a dirty, unpainted, vintage Chevrolet taxicab with a cracked windshield. I could either take the taxi or go back to Trujillo on the next bus, so I opted for the one possibility to reach my destination. After making the necessary financial arrangements with the driver, we left for the desert of Magdalena de Cao, another 20 miles up the coast. I didn't think we would make it, but an hour later we arrived. From Magdalena de Cao, it was another half hour of grinding, shaky, dusty travel along the seacoast to the Complejo del Brujo, Complex of the Witch.

One look at the tops of the three impressively large Moche huacas, truncated pyramids showing through the haze, surrounded by miles and miles of burial grounds, and I knew the trip was worth every bounce and sore muscle.

The three pyramid temples, Huaca Blanca, the white pyramid, Huaca Prieta, the dark pyramid and Huaca Partida, the split pyramid (cut in two by an earthquake a millennium ago) slowly became more and more visible as the midday sun began to disperse the heavy mist rolling in from the ocean.

It was at the Huaca Blanca that Peruvian archaeologists

Moche ceramic vessel, a prisoner, courtesy Museum of Anthropology and Archaeology, Lima

The author atop the Huaca partida (split pyramid) Magdalena de Cao, Peru

Huaca blanca (white pyramid), Magdalena de Cao desert

Moche erotic pottery figure, courtesy National Museum, Lima

Mummy of Moche woman, courtesy Museum of Archaeology and Anthropology, Lima

Moche burial site, Complejo del Brujo, Magdalena de Cao, Peru

Huaca Partida, pyramid split in two by an earthquake, Complejo del Brujo

have recently excavated 140 mummies of Moche royalty, priests and warriors, as well as a frieze-decorated wall covered with eight-foot-high, multi-colored anthropomorphic faces.

It was my great fortune and privilege to be there precisely during the time when they were digging out the shroud-wrapped mummy of a warrior, with an oxidized copper-tipped spear at his side. The 2,000-year-old mummy in a sitting position was discovered leaning against the reclining body of a woman. She was also wrapped in a cotton shroud, except that her head was exposed, and her skull with its long black hair still attached was in complete view. The warrior's head, like the rest of his body, was firmly wrapped with stitched welts of woven cotton cloth forming a circle around his face.

I was able to see clearly where the warrior's arms were folded beneath the shroud, yet there were additional, artificial arms attached to each shoulder. These false arms were made of thinly-rolled sheets of copper, over which cotton cloth had been wrapped, and at the ends, smaller rolls of copper were attached as a semblance of fingers. The false arms were raised overhead, with the outstretched fingers reaching upward, looking at first glance like a bunch of small dead branches cut from a tree.

The Moche and later the Chimú, both employed a unique method for the burial of royalty. The warrior-priests and other rulers were not placed in direct contact with the earth, as they usually buried the populace, but instead were put into niches, under platforms within the pyramids.

These niches, usually 3x3x5 meters, were dug out and filled with sand. Adobe brick was cemented over the sand. When the adobe dried, the sand was removed, leaving the bricks to act as a platform over the hollow which formerly held the sand. The sides of the enclosure would then be covered with additional adobe bricks, thus forming a niche below the surface of the huaca. By protecting the bodies of royalty, the Moche and Chimú also protected the fine ceramics which were buried with them, so that the pots and clay figures were not crushed by the weight of sand or the shifting of the earth which took place over the centuries.

I spent several days studying the Moche remains at the necropolis of the Complejo del Brujo, days during which I felt I had somehow travelled out of the real world to a place which existed only in my imagination.

The Moche, also called the Mochica, were the consummate warriors. Although most of the pre-Columbian societies had soldiers and did battle with their enemies, none can be compared to the Moche. The Moche stand out far above all of them as the most aggressive, hostile masters of conflict.

They settled in the coastal desert area of Peru, further north than the Chimú and 800 years earlier. The Moche ruled their land from 200 B.C. to 700 A.D., and during those 900 years dominated thousands of square miles of territory. They disappeared 150 years before the arrival of the Chimú.

The Warrior Priest

Why should the gods be so angered? Never have I heard such thunder from the heavens. Never have I felt the earth shake so fiercely, nor, seen darkness during the day. The sea moving northward along the coastline has turned hot, causing the fish to die, leaving a terrible stench.

What horrible things are taking place! How have I

offended the gods? What can I do to appease them so that this worst of all nightmares will cease? I have always obeyed the laws and the ritual. I have always made the correct sacrifices, and I have always instructed our lord in the ways of the sun-gods who preceded him. Just this day did I not sacrifice ten captives to assuage the hunger of the gods? Indeed they must still be hungry for the blood of sacrifice to act in such a terrible manner against us.

The people have come to tell me that the seas are rising so high upon the land, the canals are in great danger of flooding. They are asking me for a way out of this tortuous revolt of the earth and sea. How can I help them? Should I not first save myself? Should I now flee this place where the gods are moving the earth beneath my feet? No, I cannot leave this, my whole life behind. This horror will surely come to an end soon. After all, am I not invincible? Am I not the warrior priest of the Temple of the Sun!

Archaeological evidence shows that the Moche were wiped out by disease and starvation, the result of earthquake activity along the eastern side of the Pacific, which caused serious flooding and disastrous damage to crops.

The fierce fighters of the Moche were led by a warrior-priest, whose personage combined the roles of commander and spiritual leader. He was an omnipotent god-figure, holding immense power over the entire populace. During recent years, tombs of Moche rulers have been unearthed, among them the tomb of the Lord of Sipán, a warrior-priest. His extended skeleton was found with large amounts of gold, silver and turquoise jewelry, with the skeletons of his wives and slaves buried alive.

The Moche ceramic pottery describes their society in great

detail, and much that is known about them comes from these richly-decorated vessels buried in the tombs. The pots are carved with sculpture which displays their social order and all aspects of their culture: rulers, farmers, fishermen, soldiers, builders, and women going about their daily tasks. Musicians, soothsayers and prisoners of war can be seen. The vessels show an abundance of fruits and vegetables which were grown by the Moche, with corn predominating. Weapons and musical instruments are depicted.

The Moche were without a doubt the cruelest of all pre-Columbians. The prisoners taken in battle were paraded in front of the populace, naked, with ropes around their necks, and were later garroted as sacrifice. There is a ceramic piece on exhibit at the Museo de la Nacion in Lima, showing the tied-up figure of a prisoner whose facial skin had been peeled off, and whose one remaining eye is being plucked out by a large bird.

Discovery of Corn

The men were taking the boats down to the sea for the day's fishing, and the women were on their way to the fields to gather berries. One allowed the infant to suckle at her breast a while longer, until it was overtaken by sleep. She then went out past the small clearing of the village to join the others. The sun began to warm the air, and the scent of ripening berries told of good pickings for the morning. She shifted the weight of the child in the sling on her hip, as she met up with two other women, and joined them in their bird-like chattering, a ritual of sound used by the women to protect one another from danger while working in the fields. Just as the men during the hunt communicated only with the language of eye movements and gestures, the women made constant noise while gathering, to frighten away the wild animals.

They remained until the sun rose high. Their clucking sounds began to die out, as one by one they left the field. Her own basket was completely filled, when something caught her eye. A strange-looking wild plant, growing tall, only one, at the edge of the field and partially hidden by the berry vines. She approached it with curiosity and expectancy. What was this wild-growing plant with heavy tuberous offshoots halfway down its thick stalk? Was it edible? Could it be a sweet fruit, or was it bitter, would it burn the tongue? She hesitantly gathered one of the shoots and peeled back its husk to reveal neatly-arranged rows of shiny yellow kernels. She picked off one of them, and another, and crushed them between her fingers. Slowly she put her fingers to her mouth.

Erotic Ceramics

The Moche produced quantities of erotic ceramic vessels. Some depict men with an exaggerated, oversized, erect penis. Others show couples in the act of coitus. Besides the many vessels showing normal copulation between men and women, there are those which graphically display people performing acts of oral sex and sodomy, both homosexual and heterosexual. There are many vessels showing a woman seated next to a shroud-wrapped, skeletal figure of a man whose aroused sexual organ is exposed.

Through their pottery, the Moche suggest that they believed in a sexual connotation with death; perhaps they deduced that man's life was depleted through the sex act. All the evidence uncovered points to their belief that reproduction was a gift of the gods. The pre-Columbians did not connect procreation with copulation. They believed that a child was placed in the womb by one of the gods, or perhaps was a reincarnated spirit which entered the body of a woman. On some of the pottery, Moche women are displayed in various stages of childbirth, sometimes assisted by a midwife.

They produced large numbers of portrait ceramic vessels, bowls with life-size sculptured heads. The moods of the people are dramatically shown, with the many different facial expressions of sadness, joy, bewilderment, pleasure and pain. They displayed many illnesses including tumors, thyroid conditions, cleft palate, swollen jaws, hunchback, and clubfoot. Many ceramics show entire human figures mounted on top of the pots. One pot shows a man exposing his anal region to another for close observation of a bad case of hemorrhoids. One ceramic piece shows a man who evidently had a venereal disease, his body, including his limp penis covered in oval-shaped sores.

Everything concerning the lives of the Moche was shown on their ceramics preserved in the ground in the prevailing dry atmosphere of the region. Most of the pieces look as though they had just been fired, with color and glaze intact.

The weather on the northwest coast of Peru is unlike any in the world. It hardly ever rains and the ground remains dry all year. The Humboldt current brings cool air from the south, and when this air mixes with the warm air from the inland tropical area, mists form, obscuring the sun for part of the day bringing cool nights and cloudy mornings. The sun blazes forth around noon every day, perfect weather for agriculture. Yet the ground is desert-dry and along the coast consists mostly of soft, fine sand, excellent for the preservation of ceramics.

The flat-topped pyramidal huacas are the monumental mausoleums of the Moche and are spread over many miles along the coast of Peru, mostly around Trujillo. The Huaca del Sol and the Huaca de la Luna (pyramids of the sun and of the moon) which lie on a windy plain near Trujillo, are the two largest built by the Moche. The Huaca del Sol is an imposing 175-foot-high structure said to contain 160,000,000 adobe bricks. It involved thousands of people and many years in its construction.

The builders of the huacas marked many of the adobe bricks with number signs in the form of dots and lines, evidently to keep a record of their work, since much of it was performed as a tax payment. Many bricks show the indentations of four fingers and a thumb, where the worker inserted the tips of the fingers into the wet clay, to mark it permanently.

Warrior-priests and other members of the nobility are buried inside the Huaca del Sol y Huaca de la Luna, near Trujillo, but to date no extensive excavations have been undertaken. Surrounding them on all sides and extending over the desert for large distances is the necropolis, burial ground of the populace. Today they look like the surface of the moon in miniature, pockmarked with holes dug by huaceros, grave robbers who have looted the tombs for the gold, silver, and ceramic pieces.

Thousands of open graves surrounding the Huaca Blanca at the Complejo del Brujo reveal skulls and bones disturbed to obtain the treasure with which they were buried. Long strips of the woven cotton shrouds once wrapped around the mummies are now partially attached to their skeletons, partially buried in the sand. These ghost-like wispy white cloths stir in the breeze which blows constantly across the desert from the nearby sea.

From the truncated top of one of the huacas nothing disturbs the view of this exquisite, blue coastline, whose white breakers extend almost to the horizon; low, rolling breakers which continually move towards the beach in a non-ending pattern. But the sea was not always this peaceful. At the time of El Niño, around 700 A.D., it rose above the land to such an extent that it wiped out an entire culture.

Today, much of this land is covered with sugar cane plantations, said to be the largest in South America. At the time of the Moche it was all planted in corn. Underground streams, runoff from the Andes foothills, provided irrigation for thousands of acres of cornfields. Just eight degrees south of the equator, it has a climate of year-round afternoon sunshine and cool mornings and nights affording ideal weather for the cultivation of this cereal crop. And as the Moche population expanded, so did the need for larger and larger harvests.

The Moche were fundamentally fishermen, and fish, corn and other cultivated crops provided a very nutritious diet. As with the Chimú, something happened to change this ideal situation drastically. Once again El Niño struck the coast of Peru. It is known to scientists that about 700 A.D. the Humboldt current turned warm, killing the fish and other sea creatures. Flooding destroyed the irrigation system and their crops were depleted. Once again, because of agricultural expansion and overpopulation, a people could not combat the forces of nature. Once again a culture was destroyed because of overpopulation and overdependence on agriculture.

There are no geological references to prove what happened to cause the disappearance of the Moche, and a definite date has not been established. However, we do know the extent of the frequent earthquake damage along this coastline and the force of El Niño. With their basic food source gone, the Moche, like the Chimú 150 years later, ravaged by starvation and disease, simply disappeared.

INCA

The Sun Worshipers

THE INCA
Atahualpa, the Sun God

On the evening of November 16, 1532, the sun set on a great Peruvian pre-Columbian culture. When it rose the next day, the Inca empire no longer existed. One of the most splendid ancient Indian societies had disappeared.

The arrival of the Spaniard was not unexpected. The Inca priests had foretold that white gods would arrive from across the sea on winged ships, and they did come, at a time of great conflict between two factions of the royalty for control of the kingdom. The Spanish came — strangers firing blazing thunderbolts from wooden shafts held to their shoulders, dressed in shining metal — tall, bearded, bold and menacing. At first, the Indians, who had never before seen a horse, thought the mounted Spaniard was a swift, powerful, four-legged creature, not two separate beings.

The Spanish attacked at Cajamarca with only 130 foot soldiers and 40 cavalry — man-beasts, thunder-gods who had come to claim the lands and its riches. Atahualpa, the last of the Inca kings, the Sun God, was convinced of his invulnerability. Attired in a cloak and headdress of beautifully colored feathers, resplendent in gold and turquoise jewelry, surrounded by his personal guard and thousands of his army, he was carried by his bearers to the plaza of Cajamarca to meet the invader.

The parlay between the Spaniards and the Inca priests did not take long. Pizarro ordered the cannon to be fired into the ranks of Atahualpa's guard. The Inca could not withstand the booming voice and destructive power of the white god. Thus began the demise of a culture.

Francisco Pizarro, the conqueror of Peru and destroyer

of one of the great pre-Columbian civilizations, was the illegitimate son of a Spanish hidalgo and in his youth had worked in Spain as a swineherd. He was illiterate and completely uneducated, yet he was a formidable soldier. He had come to Hispaniola to join one of his relatives, Hernan Cortez, who at that time was secretary to the governor of Cuba. In the year 1519, from Cuba, Cortez launched his plan to attack the Aztecs. It was from Cuba that Pizarro came thirteen years later, via Panama, to Peru.

Pizarro took the Inca king Atahualpa captive and set the ransom at a room to be completely filled with gold. It was not long before the people complied, stacking the enormous room with gold figures, ornaments, cups, vases, plates and jewelry having an intrinsic value at the time of more than $30,000,000. This would have brought an incalculable price today, if the artistic and historical value of the pieces were taken into consideration. Nevertheless, with complete disregard for the artistic creations of the Inca, Pizarro ordered the Indian goldsmiths to melt everything into bars stamped with the seal of the crown and loaded in the holds of his ships for transport to Spain.

Later the Spaniards tried Atahualpa for treason, having accused him of fomenting a revolution and causing the death of his own brother, Huascar. The Inca emperor was found guilty and Pizarro ordered his execution, declaring that first he must be baptized. Atahualpa, descendant of the Sun, King of all the Incas, the mightiest of the pre-Columbian rulers of South America, was baptized with the name Juan, executed and given a solemn church burial.

One year later, Pizarro attacked Cuzco, the Inca capital. There in the grand plaza of Sacsahuaman, Manco Copac, the son of Atahualpa, offered resistance to the attackers, but he also was defeated, and all of Peru was declared the property of Spain and the capital established in Lima. With his mission accomplished, Pizarro set sail for Spain, and upon his arrival in Madrid one year later, he was named Marquis of Atavillas.

Once again, a people's absolute confidence in religion caused their downfall. A society of 5,000,000 people who believed that their gods would always protect them, and what is more, believed that their powerful ruler, Lord Inca, who was himself a god and a direct descendant of the Sun, would personally see to it that no harm came to them.

Who were those Incas, and how was it possible that the Spaniards, with such a small group of men could so easily defeat an army of thousands, subjugate a society and destroy a civilization?

A study of the beginnings of the Inca culture, between the years 1000 A.D. and 1300 A.D., shows that the Inca had conquered the Nazca and what was left of the kingdom of the Chimú, becoming the undisputed rulers over Peru's entire coastal desert region, its Andean highlands and tropical forest, a vast territory which required constant overseeing. Being skilled organizers with a large and willing populace of workers, the priests and administrators easily accomplished control.

They quickly learned not to destroy the people they conquered, but instead to assimilate the best of their cultures into their own, and in effect to borrow what they needed from their former enemies. The quipú, the knotted-string counting device was taken directly from the Chimú, without improvement. This became the Inca tool for inventory and collection of taxes called the mit'a. Through the use of the quipú they could tally the production and storage of corn throughout the land. A study of quipús left by the Inca gives important historical data about their culture. This was a society which, unlike the Aztec, did not have a written language, but the quipú has provided archaeologists with the means to determine the extent and population of the Inca empire.

The Inca were the best planners of the South American pre-Columbians and were builders par excellence. By far, the most impressive work left behind by the Inca was their fine stone-fitted architecture. In this they were innovators, and had no equal in Latin America. Instead of using adobe brick, as did the Moche, the Chimú and the Nazca, they constructed everything of stone — immense, extremely heavy, smoothly shaped grey-blue stone, precisely cut from large boulders and painstakingly hauled to the construction sites.

The means by which they built the trapezoidal walls for their living quarters, storage facilities and temples with stones which individually weighed up to 50 metric tons, and measured 20 feet square, is yet to be fully explained. How these were transported is not exactly known, nor how they were set in place, nor how they fitted one stone to another, so precisely that a sheet of paper cannot be inserted between them — all this without the use of mechanical lifting devices and without mortar.

They did not construct walled cities as did the Chimú. The strength of the buildings themselves, and the manner in which they were laid out precluded the need for walls. If there were any danger from attack by outside forces they simply retired within the buildings, which in themselves were the best of fortifications.

The capital of the Inca world was Cuzco, which in the

Quechua language means the navel, or in a manner of speaking, the center of the universe. It was actually a hub for the famous network of Inca roads. Cuzco today is a functional Andean city, 12,000 feet above sea level, with all the Inca structures standing and with some of them converted to modern use. The Coricancha, the Temple of the Sun, is in the heart of the city, and upon its Inca stone foundation the Spaniards built a cathedral which has stood for 500 years and is still in use. The city was built in the form of a jaguar with the fortress of Sacsahuaman as its head.

Fifty miles northeast of Cuzco, the Inca city of Machu Picchu overlooks the rapids of the Urubamba river which winds though the jungle, 7,000 feet below. Only discovered in 1911 by the American archaeologist, Hiram Bingham, Machu Picchu, which fortunately the Spaniards never found, was not mentioned in the chronicles of the conquest, retaining an undisturbed picture of a self-sustaining, fortified Inca city. This is the only place in the entire Inca realm where a protective wall was built, which proves that the city was laid out as a defensive unit, blocking the access to Cuzco. Why the Spaniards never went there remains a mystery.

Although the Inca did not have a written language, we know more about their way of life in their capital city of Cuzco than we do about all the other South American pre-Columbians, because the Spaniards brought scribes with them who recorded everything concerning the conquest. Not only was the Inca society described in words, sketches were made of their clothes, homes, agricultural systems, irrigation methods and their fabulous roads and architecture. Their family life, work habits and religious ceremonies were all minutely recorded.

The basis for the Inca empire was agriculture, and as the pre-Columbian societies which pre-date the Inca, they were dependent on their crops for sustenance. They planted corn and potatoes, grew cotton and developed a complex, sedentary, agrarian society. The populace consisted of the farmer-soldier, who did all the work in the fields and who could be called upon when there was a need for military action to conquer new lands.

Religion held all this together, through the control of the priests, who acted in the name of the ruler, the Lord Inca. The people were taught the need to supplicate the deities, who provided the rain and sunshine, and whose favor was evoked through huacas, pottery making, sacrifice and prayer.

The Inca was ripe for conquest. The Spaniard could not have arrived at a more opportune time. Civil strife had torn apart the empire, and the religious belief of the people combined with a mass reaction of awe and acceptance of the conquistadores as returning gods all contributed to an easy victory for the invaders. The city of Cuzco, in the Peruvian Andes, 12,000 feet above sea level, is the ancient site of the Inca celebration of the Inti-Raymi, the summer solstice, the day of the year the sun is at its greatest distance from the Earth, and when it provides the most daylight. For the Inca, on this day the sun was reborn, and this had to be observed by the entire populace, under the direction of Lord Inca and the supervision of the priests.

Sacsahuaman — Sacred Fort

Now, 500 years after the conquest of the Inca empire, the Quechua-speaking people of Cuzco still celebrate the arrival of the solstice. Each year, in the early cold morning hours of the 21st of June, the men, women and children of Cuzco and its surrounding areas, dressed in colorful alpaca wool ponchos and knitted earflap hats, gather together at Sacsahuaman, the large Inca fortress above the city.

Sacsahuaman covers a vast plain which served the Inca as an arena and the setting for the many religious ceremonies ordered by the emperor and supervised by the priests. The main entrance through the walls of Sacsahuaman was constructed with a trapezoidal doorway set into the huge stones, beneath which the people passed on their way to the observation areas.

They still come, through the same trapezoidal doorway, tens of thousands of Cuzqueños, the men with small colored feathers tucked in their hair on the backs of their heads or in their wide-brimmed felt hats, the women wearing bowlers, their babies carried in slings over their shoulders, and the children climbing up the stones to reach a good spot for viewing, all trying to get there before the sun rises above the horizon.

Invariably the sun arrives at 6:00 A.M., and it appears right in the middle of the trapezoidal entrance way. The Inca precisely calculated the construction of the doorway at the exact spot above the eastern horizon where the sun makes its dramatic appearance. It rises quickly, bursting above the stone doorway, sends its rays over the entire floor of Sacsahuaman and then climbs and paints the facing of the stones, lighting up the colorful garments of the people, the platforms decorated with flowers and dried corn, and brightly reflecting off brass musical instruments.

Soon, one of the elders places a large conch shell to his lips, and blows three, loud, mournful notes, calling for the start of the ceremonies — the sun has been reborn.

Trumpets and tubas blare the opening notes of a march to the accompaniment of kettle drums, snare drums and castanets, inspiring the young people to begin their dances on the platforms. Blending with the harsh brasses and percussion instruments, the quena, the Quechua bamboo flute, sounds its high-pitched haunting tune, calling the colorfully costumed dancers to perform.

The day before, a huge parade, lasting several hours, takes place in the main plaza, followed in the early evening by the procession from the Cathedral of Cuzco. Carrying lighted candles, these Quechua-speaking people of the Andes, the Indian inheritors of pre-Columbian culture, descendants of the Inca, walk slowly beside the wreathed and painted statues of saints in their flower-lined, glass-enclosed cases.

It is a solemn procession, accompanied by solemn music, yet many of the marchers have smiles upon their faces, Indian faces which reflect the flickering light of the candles held in their hands. As holy images are borne from the cathedral, perhaps some remember that 500 years ago, their ancestors carried the Lord Inca, descendant of the sun, to the plaza of Cajamarca, to meet the Spaniard.

NAZCA

The Mystics

NAZCA
The Mystics

Peru has found a perfect solution to overpopulation. Placing babies for adoption outside the country has become a widespread, flourishing business, and lately the hotels of Nazca and Ica are filled with prospective parents from many parts of the world. Little, dark-haired Indian babies, descendants of the ancient Nazca, lovingly nestle in the welcome arms of their new mothers — fair, tall, robust women from Maine and Minnesota. Bewildered new fathers from Naples and Madrid with elegantly dressed wives hurry with blanket-wrapped babies from one government office to the other. Caucasian women alongside their striding husbands, try to keep up with them, with concerned glances toward the pink and blue bundles in the arms of the men.

Like all the countries of the third world, Peru has a low per capita income and a high birthrate. I was told that it takes about two months and $10,000 to process an adoption. A little of this money may get to the biological mother, if she is known (many new-born babies are left at hospital entrances in the middle of the night) but most of it goes to lawyers and agencies. The baby-adoption business has not improved the standard of living.

Nazca, located 200 miles south of Lima, is warm and dusty during the day, with busy, overcrowded streets, small plazas surrounded by ever-present churches and a marketplace with sidewalks strewn with old paper and discarded fruits and vegetables. After dark, Nazca becomes cold and deserted. Unlike Lima and Trujillo, which are nearly always clouded over, the night sky of Nazca is clear with the constellations visible all year 'round.

The cloudless skies above Nazca presented the pre-Columbians with a splendid display of stars and planets, all of which had an important effect on the lives of the people. The movements of the constellations governed their planting and harvesting decisions and were also the principal source of mystic beliefs.

Mysticism was augmented by the use of hallucinogens. The coca leaf and star cactus (these designs are represented on the ceramic pottery) were used by the priests to produce trances and the ability to communicate with the spirit world. The Nazca did not build large cities and pyramid temples (huacas) as did the Chimú, yet there are strong similarities between the two cultures. They both used hallucinogens; they both developed techniques for the deformation of the skull, and they both practiced trepanning. Right after birth, the child's head was placed between two boards, joined at one end to form a V, and tied in place, forcing the skull to grow in an elongated shape. They also placed a pellet, suspended from a string tied around the head between the eyes above the bridge of the nose, so that the eyes would focus on the pellet, resulting in a permanent cross-eyed condition. Elongated skulls and crossed eyes were considered signs of beauty, especially among the royalty. Trepanning, the surgical lifting of small sections of the skull for the removal of tumors, is evident on many of the unearthed skulls of both the Nazca and the Chimú.

The Nazca had a primordial concern with a lack of water, and they built a complex underground aqueduct system which crisscrosses the Nazca Valley, to control the flow of subterranean water emanating from the Andes for the irrigation of their fields. This system still exists, plus an above-ground series of canals which is partially used by present-day farmers.

Ten miles from modern Nazca, in the middle of a desert of windswept sand dunes, is Cahuachi, the remains of the ancient city of the pre-Columbian Nazca. Here, under a brilliant sun, their exposed graves can be seen, over 5,000 of them looted by huaqueros seeking the treasures buried with the dead, a necropolis of open tombs, with skulls, bones, and disturbed shrouds, even baby skulls with deforming boards still attached, and scattered everywhere, among the graves, thousands of painted ceramic shards.

It is the year 500 A.D.   A Nazca woman speaks:

Such a beautiful day of excitement and joy...Oh, if I were a bird and could fly in the sky and look down upon our land today! All the women of the weaving pavilion will be honored before the gods. It is true that we deserve this honor, for have we not worked diligently spinning the cotton into yarn, making the strands very long, so that the burial shrouds will be smoothly woven and free of ugly breaks? Have we not woven large quantities of dyed colorful fabric to be sewn into the garments worn by the priests?

How I love this place, where I have worked since I was a little girl and where my own children will be instructed when they are old enough. Here I was taught the secrets of the loom, and how to fashion the intricate designs for the cloth of the mantas, those marvelous cloaks worn by the elders. Here I learned to spin the cotton and the wool of the vicuna, and how to dye yarn into the bright and beautiful colors so admired by all.

The times to come will be good indeed, with successful corn harvests and with fine weather for the planting of cotton. Did we not dig up the hollow, clay figure of the llama from under the northwest corner pillar of our house, and did it not show that the level of the chicha placed in it at the time of the last harvest had not gone down at all? Wasn't this the best omen? Everyone knows that if the level of chicha had fallen — may the gods forbid! — we would have been faced with great difficulties and poor crops. But no, the level of the chicha was high and all portends well.

The men are leaving once again to walk to the far slope of the valley, where they will continue the work of digging into the hard, crusty surface of the earth to create the long line. The marvelous line which will stretch out for many, many paces and reach beyond the horizon. And when this line is completed, it will form a gigantic needle, pointing directly at the weaving pavilion, and it will say, "There they are, the honored ones." Another line will then be dug, crisscrossing over the huge needle and ending at the needle's eye, representing the cotton yarn threaded into it. All of this will be sketched onto the surface of the land, where we know it will remain forever, together with the other wonderful figures of birds and animals outlined on our pampa.

We shall never be able to look upon the entire extent of our giant needle and see it completely, nor shall we be able to go high enough to see how it points to this place. But what a delight to know that the gods, who walk among the clouds in the heavens and look down on everything, will see the great needle, see how it points to our weaving pavilion. We shall be honored for all time to come.

Sketch of Nazca lines, humanoid figures.

Sketch of Nazca lines, hummingbird

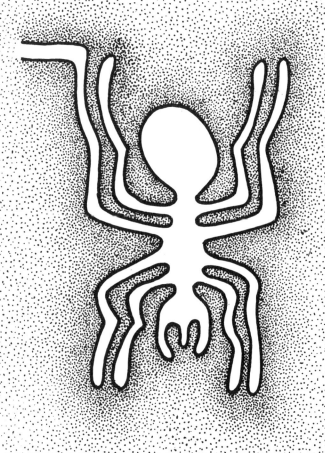

Sketch of Nazca lines, spider

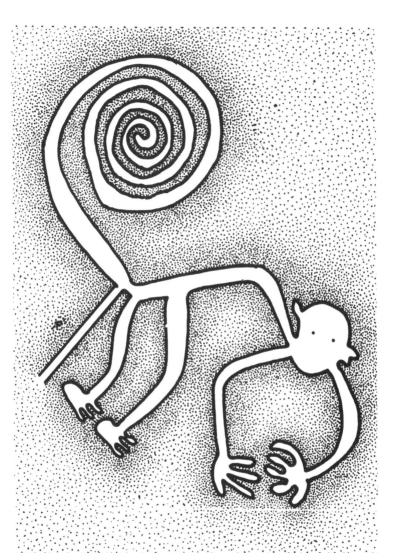

Sketch of Nazca lines, monkey

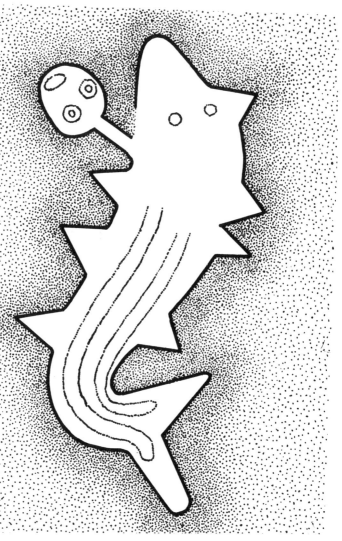

Sketch of Nazca lines, killer whale, courtesy of Museum of Archaeology and Anthropology, Lima

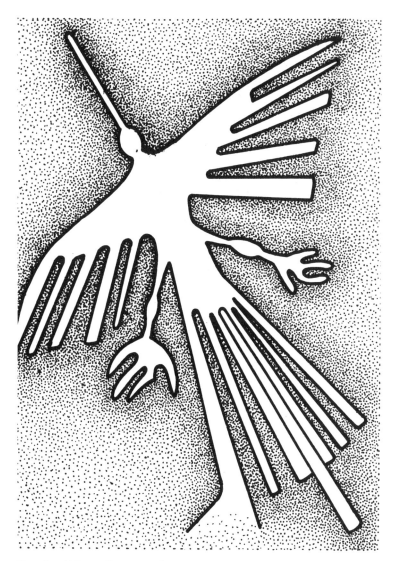

Sketch of Nazca lines, condor

Nazca ceramic, courtesy Museum of Archaeology and Anthropology, Lima

Nazca ceramic with spider & web, courtesy Museum of Archaeology and Anthropology, Lima

The Nazca Lines

Nazca culture flourished in the south coastal region of Peru around the same time as the Chimú to the north, approximately 500 to 1300 AD. The Nazca, who were also fishermen and cultivators of corn, descended from a group of hunter-gatherers who had migrated from the north to this particular area, 200 miles south of Lima, thousands of years ago. Why they chose this inhospitable, arid place is unknown. The land is barren, with hardly any rainfall, and as with the Chimú, it was necessary for the Nazca to build aqueducts to channel the underground rivers to provide sufficient irrigation for their fields.

The Nazca were not only the most creative and sensuous of the Peruvian pre-Columbians, but they also possessed an outstanding sense of humor. Nazca pottery is proof of the artistry, ingenuity and sagacity of those people. Their ceramics display excellence of design and intensity of color unique among the pre-Columbians, representing true craftsmanship and fine technique in the art of ceramics. They also display a distinctive capriciousness, evidenced by the figures painted on their vessels.

For some unknown reason the Nazca filled all the available space on their pottery. It seems as though they had a compelling need to completely cover the vessels with designs and figures. Did they have a fear of space? Did this carry over in other aspects of their lives?

Gods with thousands of attributes populated the magical world of the Nazca. These were painted on the colorful, highly-glazed vessels, along with anthropomorphic felines, bird-men, and stylized representations of people, fish, insects and the small animals of the region. Jaguars, killer whales and monkeys decorated the pots. To the pre-Columbians, the jaguar and killer whale were the powerful embodiments of gods. The monkey symbolized lasciviousness. As used by the Nazca, these exaggerated, weird, expressive figures are somewhat comparable in form to the pop art and comic figures of today.

They buried miniature ceramic vessels in the graves of children. These multi-colored and glazed vessels were grave goods designed the same as normal pots, except for their size, and it can be assumed that during their lives the Nazca children used them as toys.

Today, besides the remains of irrigation canals, the most outstanding feature of the area visible to humans only from airplane altitude are the famous Nazca lines, which are preserved due to the crusty nature of the soil and the dryness of the region.

The Nazca lines depict enormous figures of animals, birds, sea mammals and insects, as well as intricate geometrical patterns, hundreds of feet in length, etched into the dark, gravel surface of the desert. The Nazca lines have been objects of scientific study for the past 80 years. There are archaeologists who have spent most of their lives looking for a solution to the mystery of the lines, and yet, as of today, no definite logical answers have been found to the many baffling questions. There are as many explanations as there are lines.

Some archaeologists claim that the lines made by the Nazca were giant astronomical charts to predict the weather, so important in an agricultural society (especially one periodically exposed to the ravages of El Niño). This quite plausible explanation was given by the famous Maria Reiche, who lived in Nazca and studied the lines for over

40 years. She stated that the lines at one time pointed to important constellations and that the insect, bird and animal figures were representations of constellations as well.

Other believable but conflicting explanations have been given as a result of years of careful study. Paul Kosak thought the figures were religious, used by the priests of the Nazca to manipulate the people. Gerald Hawkins and a group of Peruvian engineers studied the lines in 1986. They used a purely statistical approach based upon astronomy and related the lines to the winter and summer solstice and the prediction of El Niño.

Over the years, many bizarre and outlandish explanations have been given for the existence of the Nazca lines:

1. That extraterrestrials drew the lines to act as spaceports and landing strips for their spacecraft.
2. That the lines were roads built by the Incas.
3. That the prehistoric Peruvians had a version of the Olympic games and the lines were racetracks.
4. That the lines were built by prisoners of Peruvian chain gangs serving a sentence of hard labor.
5. That the lines were a memorial to an atomic war fought thousands of years ago.
6. That they represented a huge textile workshop, where immense strands of cotton yarn, miles long, were stored to be woven later into gigantic burial shrouds.

The three most plausible explanations given to date are:

1. The Nazca made the lines to form a gigantic sky calendar.
2. They were a predictor of the summer and winter solstice events.
3. The Nazca priests used the lines to manipulate the populace.

It is quite possible that the Nazca etched those lines onto the surface of the earth for several different reasons, since they were done over many centuries, and the three above-mentioned statements might all be correct. Yet there may be other explanations. No doubt the priests were in charge of the project, because it took a great deal of organization to get any job done, and this was indeed a formidable job! Imagine the extent of such an undertaking, artists and engineers sketching lines of imaginary beasts, gigantic insects and huge stylized birds for miles and miles on the surface of the pampa, unable to see the results of their work. Bear in mind that it is necessary to fly over these drawings to be able to distinguish anything, because from ground level nothing can be seen except scratches on the earth, reaching to the horizon. Some investigators of the lines believe that the Nazca used hot air balloons to soar over the lines on inspection tours. This, of course should be filed with the rest of the bizarre theories.

Could it be that the Nazca were actually trying to communicate with the gods, who would look down from the heavens and see the gigantic drawings? Is it possible that those highly creative people were indeed playing an enormous joke on the future inhabitants of the region, leaving them something to puzzle over for centuries to come? Or did they simply seize upon an opportunity to decorate the land, satisfying an uncontrollable need to fill empty spaces, treating the earth in the same decorative manner as they did their ceramic pottery?

I believe that the mythology of the Nazca carried over to the pampa, that the lines were not astronomical, but astrological. The Nazca priests were notable astrologers who had found a zodiac in the skies, their mythology decorated on ceramic vessels with the painted figures of birds, monkeys, spiders and geometric lines exactly the same as those etched on the pampa.

The lines, drawn on the earth, done with mathematical precision, were definitely taken from the constellations. The Nazca believed that the stars had their cycles, which had to be observed to determine the best times to plant and to harvest. The giant spider, the monkey, the birds, and the other figures, served together with zigzag and straight geometric lines to register the movement of stars by which they could calculate the timing for agricultural rituals.

Astrology, mythology, superstition and hallucinogenic substances governed the lives of the Nazca. The priests, rulers at the top of the hierarchy, directed every phase of their existence until they were conquered by the Inca in the 15th century.

Although many artifacts and great earthworks of the Nazca survive, unfortunately the people did not. The few remaining Quechua-speaking farmers who call themselves Nazca who inhabit the same lands and still use the ancient canals and aqueducts to irrigate their fields, really know little about their ancestors. They profess to be guardians of the Nazca lines, but until only recently, they didn't know what the lines represented, or that there even were huge figures sketched into the surface of the land. It was not until the archaeologists arrived, flew overhead, and photographed the lines, that the inhabitants of Nazca realized what lay on the surface of the pampa around them. Stories told by the people who live there today are the same tired, bizarre tales of space stations and extraterrestrial beings, told to impress the few unwary tourists.

The Inca were to Peru what the Aztec were to Mexico —

takeover artists. Each of those empires can be compared to giant modern corporations. They were able to conquer and take over all the cultures in existence at the time in their respective parts of the world, simply because of better organization, more resources, and most important, because of their larger armies. Military conquests built the Inca empire, and the success of their armies was due to greater numbers and better supply, rather than to superior weapons. The Nazca and Inca used the same weapons, the sling, the club and the dart, and since the Inca had more men behind them, they overpowered the Nazca, a people who did not have a strong interest in war and conquest. The Inca made certain not to exterminate the Nazca, who were fine artisans and builders of roads and irrigation systems, so needed in the expanding Inca empire.

Although they certainly wanted to do so, the Inca weren't completely able to mold the Nazca into their society, because there was not sufficient time between the dates of the Inca conquest of the Nazca and the arrival of the Spanish. After the conquistadores arrived in the year 1530, genocidal warfare began, and the Inca and Nazca hierarchy were liquidated.

Nazca ceramic, courtesy Museum of Archaeology and Anthropology, Lima

Chimú skull displaying trepanning, courtesy Museum of Archaeology and Anthropology, Lima

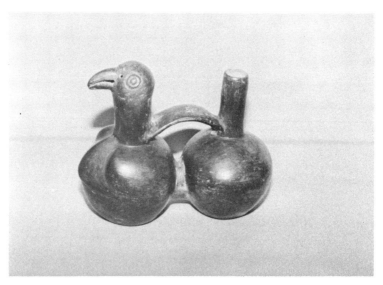

Inca-Chimú whistling pot, collection of the author

Huaca Esmeralda (Pyramid of the Emeralds) Trujillo, Peru

Chimú whistling pot, courtesy National Museum, Lima

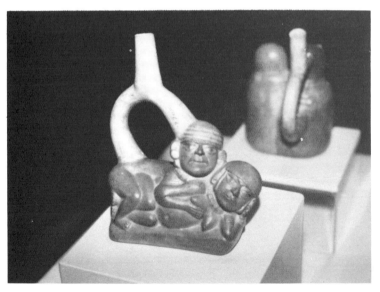

Moche erotic vessel, courtesy National Museum, Lima

Nazca ceramic, condor, courtesy National Museum, Lima

Nazca ceramic, courtesy National Museum, Lima.

Moche pumpkin ceramic, courtesy Museum of Archaeology and Anthropology, Lima

Nazca ceramic, courtesy National Museum, Lima

CONCLUSIONS

CONCLUSIONS
Pre-Columbian Indian Contributions

There cannot be a conclusion written to the story of archaeology. Dramatic discoveries are constantly being made which bring to light new facts concerning the ancient peoples, some reinforcing existing theories and some refuting them. It is a never-ending tale, with the subject matter endlessly altered by time.

The earth is the protector and preserver, covering the remains of countless cultures during the millennia — the tens, the hundreds of millennia of man's existence, the guardian of society's heritage. From time to time, Earth, like a god, gives up its secrets, and when this happens, scholars begin the process of debate and dispute over the findings and the theories advanced, and physicists and mystics, poets and theologians, anthropologists and archaeologists seek new theories to encompass the uncovered data.

In the 1800's men such as William Henry Harrison, president of the United States, and William Cullen Bryant, poet and philosopher, believed that the mounds were built by Europeans who had arrived in the Americas thousands of years ago. Neither they nor their compatriots would accept the idea that ancestors of Indians then living in Ohio and Tennessee had the capability of executing the exacting task of constructing a symmetrically perfect 100-foot mound.

However, Thomas Jefferson, scholar, architect, archaeologist, believed that Indians did build the mounds, and in 1780 excavated those near Monticello, Virginia. He arrived at the conclusion that they were giant burial grounds of Indians who had lived there centuries before. There weren't many who felt this way, and most people refused to believe in the aptitude and capability of the pre-Columbian Indian. Unfortunately, this feeling still largely prevails.

Romance is a greater persuader than fact. It is romantic and exciting to believe that ancient travellers from distant lands—Egyptians, Vikings, perhaps the lost tribe of Israel, and even extraterrestrials — were responsible for the magnificent structures of the Cliff Dwellers and the Moundbuilders, the unbelievable stoneworks of the Inca, the huacas of the Moche, the canals of the Chimú and the lines of the Nazca. It is far less interesting to acknowledge the genius and capacity of the migrant forebears of present-day Navajo, Hopi, Cherokee, and the Central and South American Indians, who built those monumental works.

Some believe that the Indians might have provided the physical labor and that other, more "advanced" beings directed the projects. These ideas are slowly changing. Now people are beginning to understand that the ancient Indians of 500 to 5,000 years ago not only possessed the creativity and intelligence, but that they actually did the planning, the inventing, the design and the building. These outstanding, unique constructions were the work of advanced, indigenous, hierarchic societies which achieved these formidable projects without the help of Europeans.

Pre-Columbian Indian Contributions

The introduction to this book deals with the pre-Columbian Indian's contribution to European culture and life-style, with the many things the Spaniards took back across the Atlantic, among which were new agricultural products, new ideas for construction, road building and irrigation of crops. What follows is an account of the ancient American Indian's imprint upon their own land, and how they influenced generations of people in the western hemisphere. It is a brief review of the inheritance the Indians left which so enriched the lives of the settlers, the colonists and the present-day population of the Americas. It is a legacy of the indigenous forebears.

Agricultural Products

Outstanding among the products given to the white settlers by the Indians were corn, potatoes, cotton and tobacco. These were to become important factors in the lives of the settlers. Based upon the cultivation of these products major industries developed, which eventually employed the labor of millions and changed the lives of people throughout the world.

Corn, introduced to the Spaniards by the Indians, is today the most widely used product in the processing of foods consumed in America. It is the single most important crop, with 300,000,000 acres of land devoted to its cultivation. During the past 500 years the cultivation of corn has grown to become a vital part of the economy of the western hemisphere. Besides its use as feed for livestock, it is milled into flour for human consumption, it is used in the distilling and fermentation industries, and it is the basic ingredient in the production of most edible oils, sweeteners and syrups. Alcohol derived from corn may one day rival petroleum as a combustible fuel. Corn is a cultigen, a product of human culture. Mass selection and cultivation by the pre-Columbian American Indians gradually transformed certain varieties of wild corn into the cultivated plant called maize.

During the 18th and 19th centuries, cotton was "king" of all crops in the southern states, its commercial growth responsible for the mass importation of African slaves. The practice eventually resulted in the War Between the States. Cotton was not new to the European conquerors. It had been cultivated in ancient Egypt, India and China. It was an important and abundant crop grown by the pre-Columbian Indians and its value was soon recognized by the Spaniards. The discovery of cotton in the New World led to its eventual exportation from the Americas to Europe and to its vast commercialization. Cotton had been grown in Mexico as far back as 5000B.C. and in Peru by about 2500B.C. The Indians of South and Central America wove cotton into exquisite textiles which so impressed the Spaniards that quantities of the cloth were taken back to Europe. Indian designs woven into cotton and wool have been copied for centuries.

The Arawaks of the Caribbean could not foresee the awesome role which tobacco plays in the world today when they presented Columbus with a few innocuous leaves loosely rolled into the shape of a cigar. Tobacco was used by the Indians as a cure for certain illnesses, in religious ceremonies and smoked as a gesture of peace during disputes. Sir Walter Raleigh began the popularization of pipe smoking in Great Britain in 1586. The Europeans were the first to convert this simple leaf into the controversial cigarette now smoked by people throughout the world. Indians from the far North and Eskimos in the Arctic received their first taste of tobacco from the British at the time of the fur trade. In exchange for furs, the Hudson Bay traders gave them European-processed tobacco leaf which ironically had been cultivated in the sub-tropical regions of the Americas.

The Fur Trade

The Indians taught the early settlers how to trap, and soon this skill evolved into one of the world's great enterprises, the enormously rich fur trade between the colonies and Europe. The Indians not only taught the colonists how to hunt animals using lures and decoys, they also taught them hunter-gatherer methods of stalking prey, outrunning, wearing down and encircling the animal. Besides the skills of the hunt, the settlers also learned the Indian skills of warfare, guerrilla warfare which the colonists employed against the British troops during the American Revolutionary War. England lost the war because its red-coated soldiers knew only one way to fight, the old European method of confronting the enemy, facing it in formation and firing from standing and kneeling positions. This proved disastrous against small groups of colonists who knew the forests, who were proficient hunters and who fought like Indians.

Natural Remedies

Many of the medicines in wide use today are made from herbs and roots which were discovered by the Indians. Rauwolfia, an extract of the snakewood plant, was brewed into a drink by the Indians and used as a calming potion. Rauwolfia lowers blood pressure and is used today to treat hypertension. Reserpine, a derivative of rauwolfia is a medicine currently used in the treatment of severe mental disorders. The leaves of the foxglove plant were brewed by the Indians to treat dropsy, an accumulation of fluids in the legs which is often the result of heart and circulatory problems. Foxglove is one of the active ingredients in the production of digitalis, today widely used to stimulate weak hearts. The pre-Columbian Indians discovered the curative powers of quinine and were the first to use coca leaves as an anaesthetic.

Ancient folk medicine is still practised by reservation Indians in the United States. The Navajos believe that disease is caused by a disruption of the harmony of life brought about by witchcraft, ghosts, or by the breaking of taboos. They use herbalists to relieve minor pain, diviners or tremblers, medicine men or singers. Ritual sweatbaths, drinking of herbal brews, and elaborate sandpainting ceremonies are employed in the treatment of illness.

Folk medicine based upon old Indian lore is practised today by the Mexican-Americans of Arizona, California, Colorado, New Mexico and Texas. The evil eye, mal de ojo, and sorcery, mal puesto, are cured by using a healer, a curandero, a shaman who employs magic and herbs to effect cures.

The ancient Nahuatl of Mexico used a mushroom which they called teonanacatl, or God's flesh, to produce hallucinations. Star cactus was used by the Nazca Indian priests to invoke trances. Coca leaf was chewed by the Incas to effect an euphoric feeling and to combat hunger, altitude sickness and as a general anaesthetic. It cannot be said that coca, after it was processed into cocaine, enriched the modern American way of life, but it certainly changed it to a great extent.

A New Botany

The Indians also changed the English language when

they provided the names which were needed to describe all the new things encountered by the white men in the Americas. Hickory, persimmon, mahogany, mangrove and mesquite are all Indian names. Yucca, maize, hominy, squash, avocado, pemmican, manioc, cassava, papaya, tapioca, succotash, scuppernong are among hundreds of Indian names for the agricultural products found. The names savannah, pampas, hurricane, chinook and blizzard were taken directly from the Indians. For those creatures never seen by white man, such as vicuna, llama, jaguar, tapir and condor, the Indian names were adopted. Quinine, curare, mescal, peyote, wigwam, igloo, teepee, poncho, papoose, cacique, powwow, potlatch, hootch, punk, honk, even the expression O.K. — all are Indian. The list is endless.

Gold and Silver

The pre-Columbian Indian not only affected the lives of the people of the Americas, but also the lives of the people in the entire world. Before Columbus most of the gold came to Europe from the west coast of Africa, and it was only a trickle, difficult to obtain and very expensive. It was not until the discovery of America that an abundance of gold began to enter Europe. The gold acquired from the Inca and Aztec and the other Indian nations was shipped across the ocean to become resplendent decorations in the cathedrals and royal palaces of Europe. Pre-Columbian gold and silver were minted into coins. The Europeans, Africans and Asians had been using coins for thousands of years, but use of coins was limited to royalty due to the scarcity of gold and silver. This changed radically when shipments from the Americas began arriving, and all the nations of Europe began minting large quantities of gold and silver coins as currency to be commonly circulated.

The Indians never looked upon precious metals for their intrinsic value. Gold and silver were worked for their beauty and ornamental qualities. The pre-Columbians did not use money as a means of exchange and therefore had no use for coins.

New World Foods

The pre-Columbian Indians radically changed the diet in most of the world by the introduction of all the new foods and spices which up to then were unknown in Europe, Asia and Africa. The potato spread through northern Europe where it was easily grown because of the temperate climate. It became the staple food in such countries such as Ireland, England, Germany and Russia, where it replaced the grains normally grown. The potato helped eliminate the centuries of famine which continually plagued Europe because of the instability of grain as a crop and its susceptibility to disease.

Sweet potato, far more nutritious than rice, became a staple food for the Chinese after its introduction there by the Spaniards. Peanuts, hot chili peppers, vanilla, coffee, cassava and many roots and tubers were taken to Africa and planted in the tropical soils of that continent, to become important foods in the African diet.

All of these foods were successfully cultivated by the American Indians at the time of the arrival of the Spaniards. With the introduction of American fruits, nuts, herbs and vegetables unknown in other lands, the diet of the entire world was changed for all time. The bowl of potato soup served in Germany, the Spanish gazpacho made with tomatoes and peppers, the Italian zucchini salad, and all the other foods which added so much flavor and zest to the European diet wouldn't even exist if it were not for their discovery and cultivation by the pre-Columbian American Indian.

Place Names

The Indians named the Americas. Names such as Dakota, Mississippi, Ohio, Illinois, Minnesota, Missouri, Arkansas, Connecticut, Massachusetts, Tennessee, Ottawa, Saskatchewan, Chattahoochee, Potomac, Tallahassee, Suwannee, Muskegon, Mohawk are all Indian. Canada, Mexico, Acapulco, Cancun, Oaxaca, and thousands more places throughout the western hemisphere were named by the Indians.

Values for Today

But the Indians tried to give the white man much more. They attempted to teach him to understand his place in nature and to teach him about the wonders of the wilderness, the land and the waters. Unfortunately the white man did not learn his lessons very well. He began very early to deplete the natural resources and contaminate the land, air and water. An outstanding example is the almost complete extinction of the beaver for the manufacture of men's hats during the 19th century fur trade.

The 20th century did not bring greater enlightenment to the people of the Americas. If anything, a disregard for the preservation of natural resources and the contamination of the atmosphere, the land and the waters increased.

The White Man's Contribution

There was a time when the ancient ones thrived in the Florida Everglades, nourished by the earth and by the waters. There was a time when they hunted and fished and planted the fields, when they flourished and their numbers grew. But now the days of the corn dance and the great tribal gatherings are past. The white man had arrived.

He came with destruction in his wake. He brought the slaves from Africa and turned the gentleness of life into misery. He worked the blacks to death in the cane fields. For a while the Seminole Indians hid and protected slaves, but this soon came to an end. Nearly all the ancestors of today's Seminoles were driven out or died of European diseases.

There are close to two million people in south Florida, nearly 1,000,000 of them living in Miami. The population is made up of Caucasians, blacks and hispanics. They converged upon these warm lands from the big, northeastern cities and from the tropical islands of the Caribbean. Some came to escape political oppression, some came hoping to get rich quickly, others came looking for a place to die. The rapidly constructed condominiums reach southwestward from Homestead and Florida City toward the Everglades National Park.

The United States government allowed millions of acres of the Everglades wetlands to be drained for dairy farms, sugarcane plantations and flood control. At one time all of the Everglades was to be set aside as a national park. In effect only one-fifth is now a national park and all the rest has been drained and cleared for subsidized agriculture and condominiums.

For thousands of years tropical storms and hurricanes have hit the Florida Everglades, temporarily destroying some of the natural things and creating opportunities for others to take hold and survive. Actually heavy rains and even floods are essential to the process of the wetland's self-renewal. The survival of this ecosystem is now dependent upon shut-off valves, pumps and human intervention.

On October 12th, 1492, there were at least 50,000 Indians living in the Everglades. On August 10th, 1992, the day hurricane Andrew tore through the area, there were only 1500 Seminole Indians living on three reservations. These are the survivors of a 12,000-year migration south over the Alaskan Land Bridge. There is no place left for them to go.

The white man placed the Indians under strict supervision and contained them within the boundaries of reservations, usually the poorest lands in a particular region. Until the beginning of the 20th century, all Indians were treated as foreigners. The Constitution decreed that the legislative branch of government had the power to regulate commerce with foreign nations, among the states and with the Indian tribes. The Congress believed it was its duty to "civilize and Christianize the red infidels." In effect, the United States Congress carried out the Indian doctrines invoked by the Spaniards three centuries earlier.

It was not until 1934 that Franklin D. Roosevelt proclaimed that no interference with Indian religious life or ceremonial expression would be tolerated. Until that time it was customary to campaign against the Indians and to influence public opinion against their religious beliefs. From the 1500's to the 1930's everything was done by the Spanish, English, French and Americans to obliterate the tribes. The Indian was subjected to forced labor, slavery,

torture, theft and kidnapping. Their numbers were so reduced by the sword, by enforced starvation and by European diseases that by the beginning of the 20th century only
about five percent of their original population remained.
Their lands had been confiscated, and although the Indian
Acts were passed by the U.S. Congress, Indians were still
relegated to the position of second-class citizens.

The Seminoles

*The Florida morning was hot and humid. James Calusa
yawned and swatted a fly that had buzzed him awake from
a restless sleep. His first thought was that today was his
20th birthday and that his teenage years were·gone. He
had to accept the fact that he was now a man and there
was no going back. He thought about this for a while,
saddened by the realization that life did not have much to
offer a man in his circumstances. He also suspected that
the dreary days ahead would not change very much from
their present bleakness. Not for a Seminole living on an
Everglades reservation.*

*He looked at his reflection in the small stained mirror
that hung over the sink and knew that he would have to
shave again. "This damned beard," he said to himself, "the
telltale sign of white blood." His grandfather had taught
him that their ancestry was Creek, originally from Geor-
gia, and that he descended from the famous chief Osceola
who had fought Andrew Jackson in the Seminole wars of
1835. There was also fierce Carib in his blood, which was
apparent in his black eyes and hair and dark copper-colored skin. He was only one-sixteenth white, but his facial
hair boldly displayed this fact to the world. This sign was*

the curse bestowed upon him by a Yankee slave trader who had raped his great-great-grandmother.

He lathered up and thought about how whites took such great pride if they had an Indian in their family tree. Yet he knew that no Indian was ever proud to have even a trace of white man's blood in his veins. He would give anything, he thought, if he could get rid of the beard forever!

The sun was now high in the sky and burning fiercely after a late-morning summer shower. The puddles on the hard-baked clay road were busy with mosquitoes which forever bred during the rainy season. In the distance he could hear the roaring of air propellers as they rapidly moved the sight-seeing boats carrying the sunburned tourists along the Everglades' canals. He pushed down hard on the starter of the Honda motorcycle, its racket blending with the noise of the boats, and sped off down the road to the junction of U.S. 41. As usual there were cars parked along the banks of the main canal, long fishing rods visible above the full pampas grasses covering the embankment. Some of the fishermen, mostly blacks, came every day to catch the wary, bewhiskered catfish.

He stopped at a sign which read "Indian Village Souvenirs" and entered a small shop which was set back off the road by a wooden walkway. His sister's voice came from the dimly-lighted interior of the shop, "Happy birthday, kid brother," she called as she came to greet him, her face displaying the first and only smile she would have for anyone that day. "Hi, Maria," he answered, bending over to give her a kiss. She was small and round, with dark eyes and long plaited hair hanging over one shoulder. She began working in the souvenir shop while still attending high school and she hated every minute of it. She hated *the white tourists, the curios and cheap trinkets, and she hated the long boring hours in the dismal, sunless interior.*

She looked forward to her brother's arrival every day on his way to work. It was how they kept in touch with one another, now that both their parents were dead, and it was a daily reassurance that all was well with them.

"How about letting me have one each of your two most popular items" he asked, and she laughed loudly as she handed him a pack of Camels and pulled a bottle of Pepsi out of the ice bin. Popping open the cap, he took a long swallow and reaching over the counter picked off the shelf a small painted figure of a dancing Indian in full feathered headdress, holding a tomahawk. He put down the bottle and plastic figure and with a loud shout began a mock Indian dance, putting one foot in front of the other, toe down first and slamming his heel into the floor boards. As he danced, he chanted a soft "Haya, ya, ya, ya, haya, haya, ya, ya."

The sound of the bell hanging over the door announced the arrival of a white middle-aged couple entering the shop and caused him to stop dancing abruptly. He turned to his sister, saying "How did you like that one, princess?" She glared at him and under her breath replied, "I don't think its very funny, Jimmy. You owe me $2.50, so pay up and get out of here, or you will be late for work. Wait, before you go, take this with you." She had prepared a ham sandwich and two oranges for his breakfast. As she turned to attend the customers, James gave her a quick kiss and left the shop swinging the brown paper bag. He placed it in the rack box of the motorcycle and went off down the road once again.

He arrived at the roadhouse a little after noon. The large sign creaked as it swayed in the occasional hot breeze, proclaiming in large red letters, "SAM'S ROADSIDE BINGO." He was in plenty of time to set the individual air-conditioning units. He began the daily ritual of sweeping up the trash dropped on the floor by patrons of the establishment the day before. He then carefully arranged the tables and chairs and when that was done, filled the soft drink machines and tested the loud speaker system. He sat down to eat his sandwich. The cool air coming through the vents had begun to combat the intensive heat.

Soon the first of the cars began arriving, kicking up dust in the sun-baked parking lot. They were early today. Cars driven by old women, their dull grey hair tied down with brightly colored headbands. Nearly all carried white plastic handbags. The men were fewer in number, all with thin white hair showing under bill caps, one hand gripping wallets inside worn polyester trousers.

Indians also came. Seminoles from Miccosukee, Hollywood and Big Cypress reservations. They arrived in swayback pickups and old motorcycles. Some who lived nearby came on foot. There were no Indian women among them. Nearly all the men wore blue jeans, boots and big cowboy hats. They would sit together around tables at the far end of the bingo parlor, listening to the caller read numbers on Ping-Pong balls, competing for a chance to get five in a row and make a few extra dollars. Most of the time they lost.

EPILOGUE
The Logic of Events

The hunter-gatherer ancestor of the pre-Columbians had no idea he had crossed a future International Date Line when he came over the Bering Sea land bridge 12,000 years ago. There was no need to calculate time, and he surely had no comprehension of dates. This changed however, when thousands of years later, the Maya and the Aztec civilizations evolving in Central America developed highly sophisticated lunar and solar calendars which were used as guides for cultivation and navigation.

Neither could that primitive traveler have known that one day the places on his journey would be named and inscribed on maps — places such as Chunkotskiy Poluostrov, Snezhnoye, Mukhomdrnoye on the Siberian side, and the Seward Peninsula, Nome, and Moses Point in Alaska. He was a nomad from Siberia, the largest land mass in the world, larger than the United States and China, an area which could easily hold all of Western Europe. That immense region was his enormous hunting ground, over which he tracked the prey from one grazing place to another.

At that time the climate on the steppes of Asia was temperate, but it became much colder, as the Ice Age froze it twelve millennia ago. The encroaching glacier drove the warm-blooded creatures out, including the big game and the two-legged creatures who hunted them.

Man did not plan the journey. He simply followed the instinctive, hunger-motivated path to survival, and it brought him to the land bridge. It was chance which took him across, as he followed the retreating herds. His journey took him through blinding snows, sub-zero cold, earthquakes and volcanic eruptions, through avalanches and over raging rivers, endless swamps.

Finally after thousands of years and thousands of lifetimes, it was accomplished — he crossed over into the New World. And on'the way he learned the many skills required to exist in his new environment, skills which enabled him to build future civilizations. He brought with him the knowledge of fire and how to control it. He learned how to make weapons and with them attained domination over all other living things. He learned how to fashion tools and how to sew skins and furs. Later came the art of weaving fiber to make cloth. From simple gathering of fruits, roots and herbs, man developed the skills of cultivation and irrigation.

He learned the medicinal properties of the simple products of the earth, and this knowledge was passed down through the ages by the priests or shaman. Strong beliefs in the supernatural were invoked — beliefs in the awesome nature gods who resided in the heavens and in the center of the earth. The movement of the planets, the stars, the sun, and the moon were recorded and interpreted. Stone structures and mounds were carefully aligned with celestial bodies. For the pre-Columbian the stars in their zodiac were portents of the future. He built huacas and temples in places where mythological events had taken place. He built the places of worship and the tombs where the gods were born, where they came forth from the earth and the sea and where they descended from the heavens.

He left behind the art of firing ceramic vessels, the art of weaving textiles and the art of working with stone and adobe. Through his artistry he spoke, telling about his life and the events which altered his life. He constructed huge cities and pyramids, mounds and temples, aqueducts, canals and underground waterways.

But since he was human, he was not perfect. He made some terrible mistakes. It is said that he "over-civilized" and in so doing lost the skills necessary to survive natural catastrophes. He despoiled the land with one-crop agriculture. In seeking more and more land for cultivation, he burned the forests and caused the soil to erode. He overpopulated his cities and eventually, he starved himself out of existence.

There are lessons to be learned from all this. It is vital that the barriers of self-interest and personal aggrandizement are broken down and the really important challenges of these times are faced. Isn't modern man making some of the same mistakes the pre-Columbian made? Overpopulation, one-crop agriculture, homogenized forestation for pulp production, increasingly widespread cattle farming, overfishing, extinction of species, and contamination of the oceans, the air, the waterways.

The inconsiderate manner in which man pursues his endeavors today has a serious negative effect upon the ecology, and in turn it will have a very detrimental effect upon future generations. It is the obligation of modern man to learn from the lessons of the decline of pre-Columbian civilizations and to correct the mistakes of the past for the well-being of those alive today and for the well-being of the people yet to come upon this planet.

Those who cannot remember the past
are condemned to fulfill it.

George Santayana
LIFE OF REASON, I, xii

Moche warrior, courtesy National Museum, Lima.

Nazca Priest with two jaguar-head serpents, courtesy National Museum, Lima

Nazca ceramic urn, courtesy Museum of Archaeology, Lima

Moche portrait vessel, courtesy National Museum, Lima

Nazca ceramic urn, courtesy National Museum, Lima

Nazca ceramic bowl, courtesy National Museum, Lima

Moche prisoner tied to a stake, courtesy National Museum, Lima

Nazca mummified head of a defeated enemy warrior, courtesy
National Museum, Lima

Nazca soldier, courtesy National Museum, Lima

Moche ceramic portrait vessel, courtesy National Museum, Lima

Moche ceramic portrait vessel, courtesy National Museum, Lima

GLOSSARY OF PRE-COLUMBIAN OCCUPATIONS

Architect
Skilled designer educated in the construction, art, design and science of building and structure. Examples:
1. Chan-Chan, walled city of the Chimú, built with adobe brick enclosures, single file walkways, burial platforms, reservoirs, food storage facilities, ceremonial halls and dwellings. (800 AD – 1200 AD)
2. Huacas, truncated pyramids built by the Moche of adobe brick, rivaling the pyramids of Egypt and the Mayas of Yucatan in size and geometric precision.
3. Cut-and-fitted stone, a type of construction of temples and trapezoidal walled enclosures built by the Inca with stones weighing up to 50 tons each, without mortar, and with such precision that a single sheet of paper will not pass between them. (1000 AD – 1534 AD)
4. Mounds, earthworks of North American Indians, constructed with thousands of tons of earth, in round, square, serpentine and rectangular shapes, the most massive and numerous structures built by ancient man in the Western Hemisphere. (1000 AD – 1300 AD)
5. Stepped, truncated pyramids, flat-topped pyramidal structures built by the Aztec and the Maya, many with tombs. (BC 2000 AD – 1527 AD)

Artist
One skilled in the arts, a means by which man records and expresses his feelings toward his contemporary world. Employed by pre-Columbians in many forms — ceramics, sculpture, stucco, metallurgy, painting and textile weaving.

1. The Nazca used up to 11 colors in painting their ceramics, creating vessels that have survived centuries of burial but look as if they had just been fired.
2. Woven textiles of the Chimú, Moche, Nazca and Inca, sewn into exquisitely colored and patterned cloths used as mantas (cloaks) and burial shrouds.
3. Frieze work of stucco and stone by the Maya, carving on the pyramids of the Aztec and glaze on the burial urns of the Barrancoid express the artistic capability of the pre-Columbians.

Astronomer
One educated in astronomy, the science that treats with the location and movement of celestial bodies. The pre-Columbians employed astronomy to predict the weather and the conditions favorable for the planting and harvesting of crops.

Hydraulic Engineer
One trained in the study of water in motion, or in the use of water pressure for power to move through narrow openings or to be transported. Employed by the pre-Columbians to build extensive systems of aqueducts and canals for irrigation of crops.

Agriculturist
One trained in the science of soil cultivation and production of crops sufficient to feed large city populations, a science employed by the pre-Columbians for planning, growing and harvesting crops of corn, potatoes, beans, squash, tomatoes, coffee, and cotton on terraced and on flat fields.

Musician
One skilled in ordering tones or sounds, in succession, and in combination, to produce a rhythmic composition

with unity and continuity. The ancient Indian cultures developed musical instruments of clay, copper, silver and wood — flutes, ocarinas, horns and drums producing sounds of excellent quality and harmony.

Physician

One skilled in the practice and art of treating for the maintenance of health and the prevention, alleviation and cure of disease. The pre-Columbian Indians treated disease with natural, herbal and root remedies. They used trepanning in brain surgery. They produced anaesthetics from coca leaf and star cactus.

Mathematician

One skilled in the science and application of numbers and their operation, used by the pre-Columbians to calculate their building and hydraulic projects, and to calculate storage needed for warehousing crops. The Inca used the quipu, a set of knotted, colored strings for addition and subtraction. The Aztec calendar was more accurate than the Gregorian calendar in use today. The Maya were the first to employ the zero, a mathematical concept foreign to the Romans or Greeks.

Shaman

An intuitive psychic healer, or spiritual guide, whose talents lay outside the sphere of physical science or knowledge. Pre-Columbians were astrologers, reading the movements of the stars and planets, communing with the gods and spirits. They invoked trances by the use of hypnosis and hallucinogens. Some believed it necessary to decapitate foreign prisoners to cause the sun to rise or to obtain some of the enemy's strength and wisdom. They employed ritual treatment of their dead, including excarnation and double burial to assure the life of the soul.

Shard form a Barrancoid burial urn from Barrancas, Venezuela

B.B. KAUFMAN

Author BERNARD BARKEN KAUFMAN was born in New York City. He became an expatriate at an early age and spent 30 years working for U.S. corporations in South America. During the years he lived in Venezuela, he produced eight documentary films; three won awards at the New York Film Festival, one a Gold Medal.

Mr. Kaufman directed the Venezuelan and the Puerto Rican sections of the Pan American Graphic Arts Program for Container Corporation of America. He was responsible for the selection of 160 artists who produced works for this annual interchange of art from 25 Latin American countries.

In 1980 the President of Venezuela Dr. Gonzalo Barrios presented Mr. Kaufman with two decorations, including the Andres Bello Medal, which is awarded for outstanding contributions in the fields of arts, sciences and literature.

During his residence in South America, he studied archaeology, specializing in Peruvian and Venezuelan pre-Columbian cultures.

In 1987 he and his wife Phyllis Rohm Kaufman left Venezuela and moved to Pinehurst, Moore County, North Carolina, Mrs. Kaufman's birthplace. Mr. Kaufman teaches pre-Columbian Art and Archaeology at Sandhills Community College, Pinehurst.

MARIUS SZNAJDERMAN

Illustrator, painter and printmaker Marius Sznajderman was born in Paris in 1926. In 1942, during World War II, he and his parents escaped from Europe to Venezuela, where he lived until 1949 when he settled in the United States. He studied art at The School of Fine Arts in Caracas, Venezuela, and at Columbia University and at Fairleigh Dickinson University.

His powerful expressionist paintings and prints have been extensively exhibited in USA and in South America. His work is represented in major public and private collections.